Relax Your Way Networking

How You Can Meet New People, Increase Your Feelings of Ease, and Create High Trust Relationships for Work and Life

(Text and Workbook)

from YourBodySoulandProsperity.com

Tom Marcoux

Executive Coach

Spoken Word Strategist

Speaker-Author of 31 books

A QuickBreakthrough Publishing Edition

Copyright © 2016 Tom Marcoux
ISBN: 0692602089
ISBN-13: 978-0692602089

All rights reserved. No part of this book may be reproduced or transmitted in any form by any means electronic or mechanical, including photocopying, recording or by any information storage and retrieval system without written permission from the publisher.

More copies are available from the publisher with the imprint QuickBreakthrough Publishing. For more information about this book contact: tomsupercoach@gmail.com

This book was developed and written with care. Names and details were modified to respect privacy.

Disclaimer: The author and publisher acknowledge that each person's situation is unique, and that readers have full responsibility to seek consultations with health, financial, spiritual and legal professionals. The author and publisher make no representations or warranties of any kind, and the author and publisher shall not be liable for any special, consequential or exemplary damages resulting, in whole or in part, from the reader's use of, or reliance upon, this material.:

Other Books by Tom Marcoux:
- Be Heard and Be Trusted: How to Get What You Want
- Emotion-Motion Life Hacks ... for More Success and Happiness
- Nothing Can Stop You This Year!
- Darkest Secrets of Persuasion and Seduction Masters
- Darkest Secrets of Charisma
- Darkest Secrets of Negotiation Masters
- Darkest Secrets of the Film and Television Industry Every Actor Should Know
- Darkest Secrets of Making a Pitch to the Film and Television Industry
- Darkest Secrets of Film Directing
- Now You See Me – Secrets of Power Networking – More Referrals

Praise for *Relax Your Way Networking* and Tom Marcoux:

• "Concerned about networking situations? Get *Relax Your Way Networking*. Success is built on high trust relationships. Master Coach Tom Marcoux reveals secrets to increase your influence."
– Greg S. Reid, Author, *Think and Grow Rich Series*
• "Tom Marcoux has distinguished himself as a coach, speaker and self-help author. His books combine his own philosophy and teachings, as well as those of other success experts, in a highly readable and relatable manner." – Danek S. Kaus, co-author of *Power Persuasion*

Praise for Tom Marcoux's Other Work:
• "In Tom Marcoux's previous book *Your Power Path to Freedom, Success and Happiness*, you learn to make new breakthroughs to feel good, get more done, believe in yourself and enjoy each day. Feel your personal energy increase!" – Dr. JoAnn Dahlkoetter, author, *Your Performing Edge* and Coach to CEOs and Olympic Gold Medalists
• "In Tom Marcoux's *Now You See Me*, the powerful and easy-to-use ideas can make a big difference in your business and your personal relationships." – Allen Klein, author of *You Can't Ruin My Day*
• "Marcoux's book *10 Seconds to Wealth* focuses on how each of us have divine gifts that we need to understand and use to be our best when the crucial '10 seconds' occur.... He identifies the divine gifts and shares how these gifts can help us create what we want in our lives, and the wealth we want." – Linda Finkle, author of *Finding The Fork In The Road: The Art of Maximizing the Potential of Business Partnerships*
• "In *Darkest Secrets of Persuasion and Seduction Masters: How to Protect Yourself and Turn the Power to Good*, learn useful countermeasures to protect you from being darkly manipulated."
– David Barron, co-author, *Power Persuasion*
• "In *Be Heard and Be Trusted*, Tom's advice on how to remain true to yourself and establish authentic rapport with clients is both insightful and reality based. He [shows how] to establish oneself as a credible expert."
- Arthur P. Ciaramicoli, Ed.D., Ph.D., author *The Curse of the Capable*
• "In *Reduce Clutter, Enlarge Your Life*, Marcoux will help you get rid of the physical and mental clutter occupying precious space in your life. You'll reclaim wasted energy, lower your stress, and find time for new opportunities." – Laura Stack, author of *Execution IS the Strategy*

Visit Tom's blog: www.BeHeardandBeTrusted.com

Tom Marcoux

CONTENTS*

Dedication and Acknowledgments	6
Use the Power of *Relax Your Way Networking*	7
Eliminate Fear and Nervousness when Meeting People for the First Time	15
Use A "Miracle Moment" to Overcome Your Fear and Achieve Your Dream!	21
Increase Your Influence—High Trust Relationships	25
The Real Secret about Making a Great First Impression	33
Find YOUR WAY to Network Better	37
Get Clients Fearlessly	41
Better than Standard Follow-up: Learn Secrets so People Enjoy Your Follow-up with Them	47
Secrets for Introverts to Do Well with Networking	57
Introverts as Excellent Public Speakers	65
How You Can Rescue Yourself from Feeling Overwhelmed	69
Final Word, Excerpt: *Darkest Secrets of Persuasion and Seduction Masters: How to Protect Yourself...*	137,138
About the Author; Special Offer to Readers of this Book	149,137

* This book includes even more material.

DEDICATION AND ACKNOWLEDGEMENTS

This book is dedicated to the terrific book and film consultant, and author Johanna E. Mac Leod. It is also dedicated to the other team members. Thanks to Barry Adamson II for editing some sections. Thanks to Johanna E. MacLeod for your insights and for rendering the front cover and back cover. Thanks to my father, Al Marcoux, for his concern and efforts for me. Thanks to my mother, Sumiyo Marcoux, a kind, generous soul. Thank you to Higher Power. Thanks to our readers, audiences, clients, my graduate/college students and my team members of Tom Marcoux Media, LLC.
The best to you.

Relax Your Way Networking

"Another networking event—I don't have the energy for that!" Helen, a member of one of my audiences said. Before my presentation, she was explaining to me that she thinks of herself as an introvert, unskillful in making new connections.

"I can help you with that," I replied. "I train people in *Relax Your Way Networking*. This is a process that uncovers YOUR WAY to ease into conversation and make warm connections. I can show you how to use what I call the *3 Rs of Relax Your Way Networking*.

REV UP (before the event)

RECHARGE (during the event)

RECOVER (after the event)."

I do not talk from theory. I need to network all the time for more sales and finding more excellent contractors in my role as CEO of a company with team members in the United Kingdom, India and USA. I've learned to build High Trust Relationships.

As an Executive Coach, I help my clients take their lives to higher levels of success and happiness.

I've helped clients prepare to:

- lead a team
- give sales presentations
- do well in auditions/interviews
- build a brand
- take a blog from zero to visitors from 173 countries
- write a first book
- start a business
- and more

Now through this book, I serve as your Executive Coach.

This Book Helps You Leap Forward for More Success and Happiness:

My work involves helping clients connect with their intuition.

I use questions and my clients experience this powerful process:

Insight—>Intuition—>Action.

With this pattern, my clients have an experience of what I call *Catapult-Moments*. The catapult on an aircraft carrier kicks the plane forward fast. With Catapult-Moments, you jump forward. You find something new and better. You experience extraordinary progress. Clarity arrives and you feel so alive!

Part of this process helps you **develop skills, strength and stamina**—all vital elements for creating more success and happiness.

I am truly happy to share with you insights and methods under the headings:
- Use the Power of *Relax Your Way Networking*
- Eliminate Fear and Nervousness when Meeting People for the First Time
- Better than Standard Follow-up: Learn Secrets so People Enjoy Your Follow-up with Them
- Secrets for Introverts to Do Well with In-Person

Networking
- How You Can Rescue Yourself from Feeling Overwhelmed
- and many others . . .

These sections are designed so you can connect with the material and quickly answer related questions.

I use certain phrases so people understand them and remember the ideas. For example, as I coach CEOs, business owners and others, I express my phrase: *"Take Command, Focus Your Brand."* Even if you don't have a business, you have a personal brand (it is what you're best known for). Your clarity makes it possible to get more of what you want in life.

Know that answering the provided questions even for just 20 seconds will give you a surprising advantage: You'll learn more about yourself and how to improve your daily actions and strategies in achieving success for your life.

Let's take the next step.

Relax Your Way Networking #1

Use the Power of *Relax Your Way Networking* for Success

"I've got some chest pain," Marvin said to his wife, Sarah. This had happened before. He got these pains just before he left for a networking event. He had gone to the doctor and been checked. The verdict? "Stress-related."

Some of us find that in-person networking stresses us out. We even avoid it. That's why I developed what I call ***"Relax***

Your Way Networking for Success, Friendship and Happiness."

I have some introvert tendencies. In talking with fellow members of the National Speakers Association, I have been surprised at how many fellow professional speakers describe themselves as introverts.

I chose each word of my phrase "Relax Your Way Networking" with care. You'll make better first impressions when you come across as relaxed. Further, you'll do better when you connect with "your way" instead of trying to use ways to be phony. You do *not* have to pretend to be an extrovert, if you're not.

We'll use the N.E.W. process

N – Nurture yourself
E – Energize before the event
W – Wonder as you connect

1. Nurture yourself

If you're an introvert, conserve your energy. Avoid scheduling a meeting before an important evening networking event. Many introverts have to "rev up" before a networking event. So take good care of yourself. Get some alone time. It does not need to be much. Every day, I enjoy music and working with a jigsaw puzzle—as part of my recharging practices.

Now it's your turn.

How can you recharge your personal energy?

2. Energize before the event

Pay attention to how much energy you really need for a networking event. For example, I tend to go to an event once a year at my alma mater Santa Clara University. How long do I stay? One hour and a half. Just by my setting my own boundary, I feel less stress.

By the way, how do you know you have introvert tendencies? If you ask immediately: "How long is the event? When can I leave?"—you probably have introvert tendencies.

Before I give a keynote address, I circulate in the audience and meet people. So I make sure to get good rest before I meet individuals—*before* I give a keynote address.

Getting refreshing sleep and eating nutritional food are important parts of your personal energy-building system.

I call this practicing the *3 R's of Relax Your Way Networking*. Let's review:

Rev up (You rest and make sure you have enough energy)

Recharge (You take a break in the middle of the event)

Recover (You make sure to get more rest and even enjoy fun ... *before* you launch into intense efforts—after the event)

Now it's your turn.

How can you build up your energy before an event? Will you get more sleep? Will you get some alone time?

3. Wonder as you connect

A number of people make themselves nervous? How? They focus on trying to impress others. When I say "wonder as you connect," I'm making an important distinction. Make a vital substitution. Throw out the focus on "impressing them." **Instead, prepare to "show them how you are impressed with them."** Wonder about how you can respond to people and help them feel comfortable in your presence.

Practice good listening skills. Rehearse asking good questions like:

- What are you looking forward to?
- What's working for you at this conference?
- How do you know our host, Mark?
- What's one of your hobbies?

Look for areas in which you share some common interests.

Here is one more technique I share in my speech "Relax Your Way Networking for Success, Friendship and Happiness" and my book *Now You See Me – Make a Great First Impression – Use Secrets of Power Networking: for More Clients, More Referrals and More Friends* . . .

- ***Sprinkle*** *a couple of details about you*

Do *not* dominate the conversation. Do not recite your resume. *Instead, drop a little hint and then ask a question.* For example, I used to wear a tie with music notes. When someone would ask about the tie, I'd say, "Oh, it's fun for me because I've written music for the soundtrack of one of my feature films." Soon after, I'd *ask the person a question* like: "What kind of music do you like to listen to?" [Remember to keep turning the conversation in the direction of the other person. **Be sure to listen to them—a lot.**]

As an Executive Coach and Spoken Word Strategist, I help my clients prepare for in-person networking events and for mingling with a crowd before they give a speech.

As a sidenote: Realize that people are attracted to *your clarity.* So rehearse how you describe what you do. Bring your comment down to a few well-chosen words.

I help my clients shift from "trying to be impressive" to being someone who makes a great connection.

I invite you to develop your process of being a great connector.

What phrases will you rehearse and memorize? By this I mean, will you rehearse your questions like "What are you looking forward to?"

_____

_____

_____

_____

_____

How will you practice the *3 R's of Relax Your Way Networking*?

Rev up (You rest and make sure you have enough energy—before the event)

Recharge (You take a break in the middle of the event)

Recover (You make sure to get more rest and even enjoy fun ... *before* you launch into intense efforts—after the event)

_____

_____

_____

_____

Tom Marcoux

_____

_____

_____

_____

_____

Relax Your Way Networking #2

Eliminate Fear and Nervousness when Meeting People for the First Time

"I just feel dread when it comes to networking events," my friend Stephanie said.

"I hear you. What specifically bothers you about walking into a networking event?" I asked.

"Oh – I'm not sure. I guess it's just so much pressure to try to impress people," Stephanie said.

For years, I have trained clients and college students in how to have Recovery Methods so they do not have to fear making a mistake when meeting people for the first time.

The major point here is that you remove a lot of nervousness, when you have Recovery Methods and avoid "trying to appear perfect."

When I teach this material in a *Relax Your Way Networking* workshop or a keynote address, I focus on this catchphrase: "Recover and Release Jitters."

We use the C.A.L.M. process of using Recovery Methods:

C – Correct "that's not what I meant"
A – Allow time with water
L – Let them help you
M – Move them to "forgive"

1. Correct "that's not what I meant"

What if you knew how to recover from any mistake in what you say? Here's a powerful method: Say, "That's not what I meant to say. What I meant to say is _____." And you tell them the correct words.

My clients report that this method is so helpful whether meeting someone new at a networking event—or even in giving a speech.

Now it's your turn.

Will you use the phrase "That's not what I meant to say. What I meant to say is ___"? Or will you modify this phrase to something you're comfortable using?

2. Allow time with water

Release yourself from having to say something immediately. Get time to think. How? Take a drink of water from a glass that you hold in your hand. (By the way, drinking water is safer than something like red wine that may stain someone's clothing.)

We notice that 40% of the population identifies themselves as introverts. Introverts like to think before they talk. The solution is to take a drink of water.

When you walk up to a group of people, you can nod and smile—and take a drink of water while you're listening to the person who is currently speaking. Then, you can find a way to introduce yourself and enter the conversation. For example, you can say, "Oh—that's interesting. I'm wondering about the XY project. By the way, I'm [your name.]"

Now it's your turn.

Will you rehearse with a friend, so that you move smoothly up to a group—while you have your glass of water in hand? Practice how you will join the conversation.

3. Let them help you

If you find yourself mispronouncing a word or not knowing how it is correctly pronounced, you might simply ask, "How do you pronounce that word?"

My point here is that *it looks worse* when someone misuses a word and continues onward oblivious to his or her error.

For example, here is how to ask for a bit of help. I have a client who has dyslexia. So when she is autographing books, she says simply, "I have dyslexia. I'll need you to spell your name one more time—a bit slower. Thank you."

Now it's your turn.

How can you gently ask for help? If you have an accent, perhaps, you might speak slower and even check in with the person to see if they heard you correctly. For example, with my clients who have accents, we sometimes switch from the word "result" to an easy-to-pronounce word: "outcome."

4. Move them to "forgive"

Many of us are afraid that we may come across too strongly.

You're supposed to be excited about what you offer (a product/service).

Still, some people may recoil. If you see the person stiffen or flinch a bit, say, "Forgive me, I was just excited that ____."

Here are examples:
- Forgive me, I was just excited that you may find this method useful when writing your book.

- Forgive me, I was just excited because it's fun to help people do _____

Now it's your turn.
Will you use the phrase "Forgive me, I was just excited that ___"?

Is there some way you want to modify the phrase?

(We avoid saying "I'm sorry" because it is less active. That is, when you say, "I'm sorry," the other person does not have much to do. Additionally, saying "I'm sorry" comes across as if one has done something really wrong. Finally, "I'm sorry" often sounds too ingratiating.)

Remember to rehearse your *Recovery Methods* and you'll significantly eliminate a large amount of nervousness. Why? Because you *know* how to adapt well—if something goes astray in a first meeting with someone.

In my interviews with top successful people, I find that they have developed ways to be at ease in first meetings with people.

You can rehearse and improve your networking skills.

(This above material is from my workshops/keynote addresses: *Relax Your Way Networking*. You can see a 1.5 min. video at YouTube.com. Type "Tom Marcoux Networking" to initiate a search.)

Which of these methods will you begin implementing?
C – Correct "that's not what I meant"
A – Allow time with water
L – Let them help you
M – Move them to "forgive"

What will you do exactly?

Relax Your Way Networking

_____

_____

_____

_____

_____

_____

_____

Tom Marcoux

Relax Your Way Networking #3

Special Note: Networking takes a lot of energy. It's vital for you to connect with your deep reason to do this form of work.

Use a "Miracle Moment" to Overcome Your Fear and Achieve Your Dream!

As I walked on the ocean floor, I took a deep breath and smiled. This was accomplishing one of my Big Dreams.

As a boy, I was thrilled by watching the Disney live-action feature film *20,000 Leagues Under the Sea*. I saw a team of men walking on the bottom of the ocean.

Later, I enjoyed James Cameron's film *The Abyss* which also included deep sea divers.

To get to the point of walking on the floor of the ocean, I had to *overcome two fears* related to *Sharks!* and to the claustrophobia of wearing a diving helmet.

Some days before my trip to the Grand Caymans, I practiced wearing a hood and visualizing that I was fine while wearing the helmet and walking on the ocean floor. *Positive visualization helped.*

I also asked about the presence of sharks, and I was informed that where I was diving sharks found the noise of various ships and the busy port to be off-putting.

Here's what I call the "Miracle Moment" to Really Achieve Your Dream:

It's the moment you connect with Something More Important than Your Fear.

Fulfilling my dream of walking on the ocean's floor was more important to me than my fear.

"Courage is not the absence of fear but rather the judgment that something is more important than fear." – Meg Cabot

Now it's your turn.
Write down your answers to these questions:

What is your Big Dream?

_____

_____

_____

What do you want to do?

_____

_____

What will *Feel Great!* to *you* as you're accomplishing your Big Dream?

_____

_____

_____

What will you be able to do that you cannot do now— when you accomplish your Big Dream?

_____

_____

_____

What fears are connected to what you need to do to accomplish your Big Dream?

_____

_____

_____

What about your Big Dream is More Important than Your Fear?

_____

_____

_____

_____

The above process is connected to what you want *to feel* when you're realizing your dream.

As an Executive Coach, I often help clients move beyond their comfort zone and to accomplish extraordinary things. I help my clients connect with Big Energy (which is heartfelt) and then they have something More Important than their fear.

Take the time to really connect with what moves your heart. Then, from this foundation, spring up and make progress to accomplish your dream.

Relax Your Way Networking #4

Increase Your Influence — the Power of High Trust Relationships

Do you want your career or your own company to leap to a higher level of success? The answer is: create High Trust Relationships.

We'll use the T.R.U.S.T. process:

T – turn up understanding
R – respect them
U – up the exclusivity
S – say their words (listen)
T – trigger new connections

1. Turn up understanding
We trust what we understand. We shy away from the unknown.

That's the reason that it's important for you to refine your words and rehearse them.

It is crucial to be brief. When a person meets you, he or she wants to put you into a category fast.

People do *not* want to endure uncertainty. In much of my writing and when someone asks me about what I do, I reply with a brief comment that includes these words:

Tom Marcoux – Executive Coach – Spoken Word Strategist.

At times, I share this comment: **"I help people create High Trust Relationships with audiences, sales prospects and team members. Then the person gets the Golden Yes!"**

Also in videos I say, "High Trust Relationships help you gain more Success and the Golden Yes!" (The rhyming is by design.)

As a Spoken Word Strategist, I help people *drop the Jitters and Jumbles in speaking.*

I further help people to *Take Command, Focus Your Brand.*

I've shared the above examples to make it clear that it helps to **have a few well chosen words** to help people understand what you do.

Now it's your turn.

How can you describe yourself and what you do in brief, powerful words?

2. Respect them

"Is this a good time to talk?" I ask at the beginning of many phone conversations. Why? Because I want to demonstrate my respectful attention to the other person's situation.

At one point, I asked my graduate students: "Do you trust someone who never admits an error or a mistake?" They replied with a resounding, "No!"

Why? The person who never owns a mistake is the one who can never improve.

Much of effective business is identifying what's not working quickly and then modifying the team's actions fast to make improvements.

Part of being a successful leader is to welcome the "tough news" and *treat the person communicating such information in a respectful manner.*

A truism is: **What gets rewarded, get repeated.** So if you want to leap forward, you need to give appreciation to those people who tell you the truth.

To get more sales, pay close attention to your buyers' experiences. *Make sure that they feel respected and appreciated* throughout the whole sales/use of your product cycle. Check in with them. Respected customers are the source of great referrals.

Respect is helpful for increasing team members' productivity. Years ago, a study showed that asking factory workers for their opinions raised productivity a lot. The workers felt heard and respected.

Now it's your turn.

How can you ask respectful questions, listen well and demonstrate that your clients/team members' thoughts and feelings are important to you?

3. Up the exclusivity

We do not trust things that are cheap. We think the item might break.

Many of us are willing to pay more for something that's worth more.

Who do people want to work with? — top experts. Are such experts available anytime you want them? No. Why? They're busy. And they're selective about which clients they accept.

Sadly, many desperate salespeople make themselves available at all times. What does that communicate? Desperation. Why does the salesperson have so much time on their hands? By the way, don't they have friends and family? Does the salesperson take no time off to recharge so they're at their best when at work?

The above includes some controversial thoughts. Still, let's look at engaging a doctor. Don't you need to make an appointment?

Also exclusivity makes us feel special.

If anyone can get into a club, then if feels like membership in that club is not as valuable.

My own company has been considering a special program in which certain clients can get access to my encouragement and strategies. It's called *Tom Marcoux's Your Power Path Private Club.* For a yearly subscription, one would get access to me via conference calls, videos, audios and a private, hidden Facebook group.

Now it's your turn.

How can you demonstrate that you're selective in accepting clients?

4. Say their words (listen)

How do people know that you're listening? They believe that you're attentive when you say back what you heard them express. A lot of authors suggest that you paraphrase what you heard.

My point is: **Sprinkle some of the person's *specific words* into what you say back to him or her.**

People often choose specific words because they have special meaning and even subconscious feelings attached to them.

Look at this example:

Prospective Client: "I'm looking for a car that shows I'm an elite member of my profession."

The *less-effective* paraphrased reply: "I hear you. You want to show that you're an important member of your industry."

Effective **Reply:** That makes sense. You're an elite member of your profession and everything, including your car, communicates that, right?

Why is it important to use the word "elite" (in the above example)? Because that word means different things to different people.

Many people who have invested several years and hundreds of thousands of dollars in their education truly feel that they're the elite: Top thinkers and Top doers in any population. Author Steve Siebold talks about the difference between "middle class thinking" and "world class thinking." This may be controversial. But a lot of people have really struggled and made sacrifices to rise up in the world.

Anyone talking to such top successful people will do better by listening closely *and saying back certain vital words.*

Now it's your turn.

Are you making sure that you're healthy and wide-awake so you can listen closely to what people are saying in words and body language?

5. Turn up connecting people

People like it when they know that you are "watching their back." How can you do that? Find out who their ideal client is and see if you can connect them with good prospective clients.

Additionally, **get known for connecting people to each other.** For example, I'll connect a professional speaker with a video editor when the speaker wants to make an updated demo-video. The speaker benefits and so does the video editor.

When I talk about "turn up connecting people," I'm also talking about how YOU connect with a prospective client.

A powerful way to connect with prospective clients is to use effective videos.

To see an example, view my video "Tom Marcoux Helps You Build Your Brand" (on YouTube.com). In just 1.6 minutes, I communicate how I can help one build a brand, and I also *tell a story* as I address the camera (the person) directly.

Stories reduce resistance.

How can you get strangers to want to talk with you? Have them see a video.

Now they know you as a person. (It's a start.) This is better than an ad.

We trust a person more than we trust some faceless company or institution.

Now it's your turn.

How can you use video (perhaps, on YouTube.com) so people can start trusting you even before they talk with you via phone or Skype?

* * *

Anything you want is probably a few steps away when you have more High Trust Relationships.

Remember to use the T.R.U.S.T. process:

T – turn up understanding
R – respect them
U – up the exclusivity
S – say their words (listen)
T – trigger new connections

Make every day one in which you start relationships well and create trust.

Then your opportunities will increase many fold.

How will you get people to know that you're trustworthy and respectful? What stories will you tell that demonstrate you're a person whom people trust? Will you say "Is this a good time to talk?" when you call someone on the phone? ... Will you consider using a video or telling stories as a way to connect with more people?

Relax Your Way Networking #5

The Real Secret about Making a Great First Impression: "Impress LESS, Listen MORE"

"What's holding you back from going to that networking event?" I asked my client Christine.

"I don't have the energy to put on a phony mask. I'm not perfect. I'm not the best graphic artist. And I don't have the energy to impress people," Christine lamented.

"What if I could help you shift the whole process? What if you could avoid putting on a 'mask'?" I asked.

"That would be a relief!" Christine said.

The metaphor "put on a phony mask" drains energy from many of us.

I'll say it in few words:

You do NOT need to put on a phony mask to create warm connections.

In fact, it's better that you do **not** try to pretend to be perfect or "impressive." Why? People see through it. They will just feel uncomfortable when near you because they pick up *your* discomfort-energy.

Instead, shift the whole process!
In my workshops, I put it this way:

Impress LESS,
Listen MORE.

Listening is the royal road to High Trust Relationships.
Further, when I say "impress LESS" — I mean, ***stop** trying so hard to impress people.*
Instead, make a warm connection.
How? We replace a "phony mask" with a "backpack."

When I went hiking, I discovered that a "well-fitted backpack" feels fine to wear. Why? It's fitted to your hips so the weight is on your hips, and you avoid a strain to your back!

So we place "Listening Methods" into your metaphorical backpack.

For easy remembering, we'll cover the Listening Methods as the E.A.R. process:

E – encourage through "gentle questions"
A – align with "I agree"
R – release tension with a "pivot"

1. Encourage through "gentle questions"
To me a "gentle question," is one that is easy to answer and, perhaps, even fun to answer.

I often ask people about their hobbies.
Gentle Questions:
- What are you looking forward to?
- How do you know our host, Mark?
- Are you looking forward to a particular speaker at this conference?

2. Align with "I agree"

Many people devote so much automatic energy to trying to convince people that they're right about something. With that in mind, see if you can say sincerely "I agree" to something that the person is talking about.

If you cannot agree, you can use the next method ...

3. Release tension with a "pivot"

When someone senses that we don't agree with him or her, some tension is created. It's important to show that you're listening and that you understand the other person's point of view.

You could say something similar to:
- I hear what you're saying. If I was a parent, I would rush to that school and make sure that . . .
- That sounds intense. That must have been frustrating for you.

One way to make a good "pivot" is to acknowledge the person's feelings. That's the beauty in my above phrase: "That sounds intense. That must have been frustrating for you."

You'll notice that I'm careful to say "sounds intense." I do NOT tell a person how he or she is feeling.

If I say, "must have been frustrating for you," the person could easily correct my impression by saying, "Not frustrating. It made me angry."

You can also make a pivot by asking a question.
You could ask something like:
- When that supervisor showed up and stopped the event, it sounds like a bunch of trouble happened. How did it go for you at that point?

This reminds me of how I often follow-up with people on

Facebook. I ask: "Janet, how are things going?"

I've learned that some people get uncomfortable with either one asking something "too personal" or even too "sunny."

I might want to ask: "Tell me something good that going on for you"—but the person may be in the middle of a messy divorce. So I simply ask "How are things going?"

If the person wants to vent for a little while, I'll listen.

Remember, you're *not* trying to impress people. You just listen. You let them shine. And *they like you for it*.

How will you rehearse? Use these elements:
E – encourage through gentle questions
A – align with "I agree"
R – release tension with a "pivot"

_____

_____

_____

_____

_____

_____

_____

Relax Your Way Networking #6

Find YOUR WAY to Network Better

"I'm an introvert! I dread going to networking events," Cindy, a new acquaintance, told me.

"I hear you," I replied.

If you're looking for a job or if you're promoting your own business, you likely need to meet new people. I tend to go to two networking events a week.

I've discovered that it's possible to bring more comfort and strength to yourself so you do NOT procrastinate on attending networking events.

Here are three questions that can help identify *YOUR WAY of networking*—so you're stronger and take action to network effectively.

3 Questions to Enhance "Your Way" of Networking

1. When do you feel comfortable when meeting a new person?

2. How can you do more of that?

3. If you need to go into a new circle, how can you bring your support?

1. When do you feel comfortable when meeting a new person?

"I feel better when I meet someone in a quieter situation. I don't like parties with loud music or meeting someone in an auditorium during a conference," one friend told me.

For many us, the answer can be: Attend smaller functions. Some people attend Toastmasters meetings. Others pick a cause and volunteer in various ways.

2. How can you do more of that?

This question, of course, ties into the first one. Still, it's a vital question.

If you want to do more of something, pay attention to what may be holding you back.

One of my clients cut down on the number of classes she was teaching so she could concentrate on building her own home-based business.

She needed more time and she needed to reserve her own personal energy so she could attend more events.

A number of my mentors have advised me that when you're offering a service, people are really *buying based on their connection with you*—that is, based on their personal trust they place in you. A fancy website, brochure or card does *not* match the value of your personally connecting with your prospective clients.

3. If you need to go into a new circle, how can you bring your support?

I advise clients to bring someone who really builds them up to a networking event. Judy, one client, brought her platonic friend Andy because he was so warm and encouraging. Just talking to him for three minutes reenergizes her.

I told her to "Make it a game you can win." She and Andy attend events. Judy goes over to a circle of people and talks with them. Then she returns to Andy to show him that she has checked off having a good conversation with two people. "Good work, Judy!" Andy says, "Just 8 more to go. Then we'll go to dinner to celebrate."

I call this process *"The search party goes out then returns to the refueling station. Then the search party goes out again."*

Judy does this pattern for no more than one hour and thirty minutes and then she and Andy do something fun to celebrate!

Write down your answers to these questions:
1. When do you feel comfortable when meeting a new person?
2. How can you do more of that?
3. If you need to go into a new circle, how can you bring your support?

_____

_____

_____

_____

_____

_____

Relax Your Way Networking #7

Get Clients Fearlessly

"You're a great coach," I said to my friend Marion.

"Yeah, but I don't have enough clients," she lamented.

"What's causing that?" I asked.

After she provided all sorts of reasons, including the economy and more, she finally confessed, "I'm afraid."

"Well done!" I said. "This is good work that you're acknowledging fear. We can build upwards from here."

As an Executive Coach – Spoken Word Strategist, I often help clients develop their brand, products, services and their sales/marketing process. I help new entrepreneurs and veteran entrepreneurs take their success to higher levels. I help them get the blocks out of the way so their prosperity flows well.

We use the A.I.M. process:

A – admit fear-points
I – intensify Fearless-Action
M – measure and connect

1. Admit fear-points

Some years ago, I wasn't asking for referrals. Why? Fear. I was afraid of asking too soon, of breaking rapport, or imposing on the other person.

It's fear that holds us back from getting our product or service into the hands of so many people who would greatly benefit.

What fear?

Let's look closely:

Fear of

- rejection
- looking stupid
- interrupting, being crude and rude
- blowing the deal with a client
- hurting one's reputation
- losing money
- wasting time

The springboard for doing well is to "admit one's fear-points."

First you admit your fear-point, then you develop a plan of action to handle that particular fear-point.

Then you go into the real world and implement the plan of action and see what works and what needs refinement.

There is an additional step in this process:

Admit Fear-point –> Develop a Plan –> Get Coaching/Rehearsal –> Take Action

Rehearsal is a prime method to help you quiet down fear.

To this day, I rehearse before a vital phone call and before attending networking events (for example).

"The key to success is for you to make a habit throughout your life of doing the things you fear." – Vincent Van Gogh

Now it's your turn.

What is a fear-point for you? How can you make a plan, get coaching, rehearse and take effective action?

2. Intensify Fearless-Action

What would you do if fear did NOT stop you? This is the Fearless-Action.

Over the years, I have told myself:
- I'd ask that best-selling author to endorse my book
- I'd ask for a referral
- I'd ask the person to pay my retainer for a whole year in advance

This is the real power of identifying your Fearless-Action: You then prepare, make a plan and implement that plan.

Now it's your turn.

What would you do if fear did NOT stop you? How can you prepare and rehearse so you actually do the Fearless-Action?

3. Measure and connect

It's true that we often cannot improve something if we don't measure it.

For example, I guide clients who see how to really improve their business:

Have Three Simple Measurements:
"This week how many times did I
- ask for a referral,
- have a "sales conversation"
- ask someone to buy something?

The important detail is: You don't move to the step of asking someone to buy without having a good connection with that person.

What does it take to have a good connection?
- Listening well.
- Quieting down your own fear about getting sales.
- Applying your full attention to this present moment.

For many of us, the above actions require coaching and rehearsal.

Now it's your turn.

How can you pick a simple measurement to energize you to make progress?

Now, back track and look at how you can improve your connection so you ask for a referral/sale at the appropriate time. How can you make sure that you're creating High Trust Relationships?

* * *

Do you need a boost to overcome fear? See this my 1.5 min. video on Youtube.com—type "Tom Marcoux Emotion-Motion Life Hacks" into the search box.

To "Get Clients Fearlessly" learn to implement the A.I.M. process:

A – admit fear-points
I – intensify Fearless-Action
M – measure and connect

What would be three Fearless-Actions for you? How can you take a small step forward in the direction of those Fearless-Actions? How can you get support so you take a Fearless-Action? (Example: one person had a friend help her with an email to a potential big time client. The friend remained on the phone all the way up to my client clicking "send" on the email message.)

_____

_____

_____

_____

_____

_____

_____

_____

Tom Marcoux

Relax Your Way Networking #8

Better than Standard Follow-up: Learn Secrets so People Enjoy Your Follow-up with Them

Some years ago, I had business cards from nine people after first meeting them at a Chamber of Commerce event.

I knew I should follow up with them. But then I hesitated. I had some disempowering feelings like: "Oh, they'll think I'm bothering them" and "They'll think I'm trying to sell them something."

Did I follow up? No. In fact, their business cards got lost in a file somewhere.

Can you relate to that experience?

Years later, I have learned how to be more skillful about new contacts and follow-up.

Do you want to truly expand your success? Learn to transform how you follow up with people. Many people simply fail to follow up because of two incomplete perceptions that follow up is "drudgery" and "bothering someone again." Stop! You can make follow up into something that the other person welcomes—and that you're comfortable doing! You will actually feel good as you do the follow-up activities.

First you need to transform "follow-up" into what I call "Follow-Good." The other person feels good while you contact them, and you feel good about the process. You stop dreading your follow-up actions. We will use the G.O.O.D. process:

G – Get ready ahead of time
O – Organize a system
O – Open dialogue
D – Do follow up in 2 minute segments

1. Get ready ahead of time
The essence of "Follow-Good" is to transform yourself from an intruder into a "host" and an "invited guest."
To do this, you need to get ready ahead of time.

For example, when I attend an in-person networking event, I bring 3x5 cards. Why? So I can take notes at an appropriate time. For example, if you are talking with someone from an Asian culture do NOT write on their business card. I hold my 3x5 card next to their card and I write notes on the 3x5 card and then place the person's card into my folded 3x5 card. Then the cards are together, and they go into my pre-selected pocket.

The above process is for you to identify what the person is interested in. This will give you clues as to what you can give to the person in order to brighten his or her life. Let's say that Sarah's daughter is taking karate classes, you can send a copy of an article that shows how girls can excel in martial art classes.

Bob Burg, author of *Endless Referrals*, emphasizes the value of sending people a hand-written follow-up card. Here is how you can get ready ahead of time.

In advance, set up your thank you cards. Have them ready to go in a #10 envelope, with your handwritten return address, and hand-applied postage stamp.

Then, the same night of a networking event, fill out the cards (which have your photo and contact information) and place the completed cards in a mailbox. [Sure, you could send an email message, but everybody does that—no one stands out.]

2. Organize a system

To do follow up effectively and with little pain, it is good to use a system. As you develop this system, think of ways for you to streamline the system into easy steps. *You need to feel good* as YOU do the follow-up work. Hence my phrase: "Follow-Good." You are actually doing a good work. You're providing a benefit for the other person.

Here is an example of a system:

1) Meet the person at a networking event.

2) Send an email the same night of the first encounter OR send a follow-up, handwritten card (in a #10 envelope).

3) Place in your calendar system a prompt to remind you to find a suitable article that might be useful to the person.

4) Print out that article and send it.

Each person will find how to customize his or her own system. Bob Burg suggests that one send a notepad with one's photo and contact information on each page.

Bob feels that such a notepad keeps you in front of the prospective client's face.

3. Open dialogue

Consider your follow-up activities as continuing a

positive dialogue with the new person. Certainly, connect with the person simply to say, "How are things going?" This works well in social media. Often, I will see that someone is online and available for a chat at Facebook. So I simply type, "Andrea, how are things going?" Then I "listen" as they often vent about something. With me, they have an empathetic ear. The person sees that I am demonstrating care and concern.

4. Do follow up in two minute segments

What gets done? Something that is easy and fast to do. You can follow up with a person in a short amount of time. For example, in 1988 a *New York Times* article revealed how movie mogul Jeffrey Katzenberg made up 600 phone calls a week. He was called "the master of the two minute phone call." Katzenberg had two secretaries who split the Katzenberg day between them. They placed the calls and had people hold on so that Katzenberg could go from one conversation to the next.

Katzenberg's example is extreme. But we can take some inspiration that it is valuable to stay in contact with people.

Here is another example. Consider having an open file carton next to your desk. When you think of a follow-up idea, jot it down and toss it into the open file for a particular person.

(You can also jot the idea down in a reminder that you place into an online calendar system.)

A really powerful *Follow-Good* practice is to jot a handwritten note down in two minutes. Later, in the day, take two minutes and get that note into the mail.

Praise people. Celebrate their day.

A while ago, I called a friend and said, "Happy today. We can celebrate that one year ago today, you finished writing your first book!"

People appreciate that you notice their special days.

Use these "Follow-Good" methods:

G – Get ready ahead of time

O – Organize a system

O – Open dialogue

D – Do follow up in 2 minute segments

Consider asking people in your networking circle these important questions:
- How can I recognize a good client for you?
- How can I be supportive of what you're doing?

When they tell you, you can get some time to consider how you might help. (I call such time "thinkspace.")

You could reply with something like: "I hear you. It would be great for me to promote your book from my Facebook wall. I need to double-check a couple of things. How about I get back to you on Thursday afternoon?"

One of my clients faced such a situation. When she got back to the person, she said, "I've found a way to be helpful. I can send out a tweet about your new book. I'm comfortable with that."

Remember, we can develop a Circle of Success.

We can actually feel good about how we help other people. We become the "host" of good things that we do—including connecting people in our network.

When you call, you will be treated like an invited guest.

This is all based on what I call "The Three Magic Words of Networking: 'Help Them First.'"

Good journey.

How can you "help them first" in terms of new acquaintances? Can you ask gentle questions and find out

their hobbies and job-related areas of interest? Can you connect people in your networking-circle with each other?

Relax Your Way Networking #9

One Magic Question:
"How can I be supportive of what you're doing?"

In the section about "Better Than Standard Follow-up," I introduced the question *"How can I be supportive of what you're doing?"*

Here I will go into more detail because I've seen clients fail to use this question due to one thing: Fear.

Where does this fear come from? — the possibility that someone may ask for too much.

Yesterday, someone asked me to sit down and listen to him give me an "informational hour." Inside, I immediately felt pressed upon since I'm in the middle of the deadline for writing this book in your hands.

My way to handle the situation was to tell the truth. I'm under deadline (with this book) and still I have some interest in what he's talking about.

So I said, "I'm not saying 'no.' Still, I need to see if this might fit in my schedule at a later time."

The truth is: As you become more and more successful, more people will want to have some of your time.

Still, do not let your fear of disappointing anyone cause you to hurt yourself! Additionally, just because you ask the question "How can I be supportive of what you're doing?"—you do *not* have the obligation to help the person in exactly the way he or she prefers. Often, you can help in a way that does *not* turn your own life upside-down.

For certain times, be prepared to say something like: "I can see your passion for your project. I'm excited for you. And attending that event [show your sadness] is not going to work for me." It's important at times to say "no" because you're saying YES to yourself for something else. You may need to use this phrase: "No, that's not going to work for me."

Some people ask me to post something on my Facebook wall. Sometimes, their message does not match what I talk about. So I might be able to offer that I'll call someone who may be a potential client for the person. So I have helped, but not in the way the person first proposed.

We'll use the C.A.N. process:

C – convey that you're listening
A – arrange "thinkspace"
N – nurture yourself

1. Convey that you're listening
You can say something like:
"I can hear how you're doing important work."
"I understand how you're really helping people."

Listening does NOT mean that you're agreeing.
It means that you hear and understand—and you're

showing respect to the person.

You do not have to agree.

Additionally, if you're distracted, do NOT try to pretend that you're able to focus.

I have said,

"This sounds powerful. I want to listen more. But I'm distracted. I'll need to step away for the restroom. Excuse me."

When someone drones on and on, I have said, "I promised my team members that I would mingle and it's been great talking with you. Oh—do you have a card?"

2. Arrange "thinkspace"

"Thinkspace" is a term that I coined to remind my clients to give themselves time and space to consider a request—and to *avoid* saying *yes* too fast! You can say, "I know how important your work is. I'll need to check with [team members, family members] to see how my schedule is around then. How about I get back to you Thursday afternoon about this?"

3. Nurture yourself

Remember, if you agree to something that you really dislike, your energy at the event will be low and you'll create damage to your connection with the person.

So a major priority of your life is to nurture yourself so that your default-energy is good and strong.

If you give away all of your prime personal energy, then you'll may build up resentment. Such resentment-energy can torpedo your relationships. Instead, be sure to avoid "overbooking your life."

I often note "I'm working with some family details." I do not elaborate because that's the business of my family members and me.

Taking good care of family (and that includes me!) is important.

The truth is: People will step back (often) when you are forthright.

What phrases will you memorize so that you can still ask "How can I be supportive of what you're doing?" Have ways to create "thinkspace" for yourself.

For Introverts—Secrets to Excel #1

Secrets for Introverts to Do Well with In-Person Networking

Are you an introvert? There are a lot of guesses and theories floating about as to what an introvert really is. Ask yourself this question: "Do you need to recharge your personal energy by having some time *away* from others?" You might have a few "introvert tendencies."

Now, we'll explore the I.N.T.R.O. process to help you gear up for networking events:

I – Invest in building your energy
N – Nurture your lines before an event
T – Target reasonable goals
R – Recover as you go along
O – Organize support

1. Invest in building your energy

Many extroverts *like* to go to social gatherings because they get a rush of new personal energy. On the other hand, many introverts hesitate about going to an in-person networking event because they feel the need to "power-up" to be ready to talk with people.

Some introverts look upon going to an event as terrible duty that they must endure to try to get business. Such an experience can be self-defeating. *The solution* is to consciously decide to take action to build up your energy. How? For introverts, time alone can be "battery-charging."

For example, I have some introvert tendencies so I find that time with music and assembling a jigsaw puzzle as relaxing and energy-restoring. Focus on whatever you enjoy doing—that builds your energy—and do it! You owe it to yourself in building a better you. Activities you enjoy to *recharge* are key in helping you succeed with opportunities that might otherwise appear daunting.

But this is not all when it comes to investing your focus and effort. Another point is: Guard your personal energy before an event. That is, avoid going to a meeting in the afternoon before an evening networking event. Take care of yourself. You really need more personal energy to be at your best at the networking event.

2. Nurture your lines before an event

What causes you to be most nervous? Is it that you don't know your words (your lines) before you step into the room of an event?

I emphasize with my clients to "nurture your lines;" and by this I mean for you to take a higher level approach: Rehearse what you will say. (Often it helps to gain coaching). With my clients on the phone, I guide them through *Dynamic Rehearsal.* I take on the role of the other person and the client rehearses how she'll speak and respond to the other person.

Rehearsal gives you a real benefit: If You KNOW that you *know* how to perform better, your confidence is enhanced.

3. Target reasonable goals

Some people have a mistaken notion that one has to stay for hours at an event and give out 30 business cards.

Instead, it's better to target reasonable goals like: "Stay for 1 hour. Have 5 good conversations. Gain 4 business cards."

4. Recover as you go along

After you complete one conversation, you might find it helpful to take a breather—a short break. You could step outside the room and get a bit of fresh air. You could get a drink of water. If you're an introvert, support yourself and realize that it is taking personal energy for you to interact with each person at the event. Take a break. Renew your energy. (This is the RECHARGE step of the *3 Rs of Relax Your Way Networking*.)

5. Organize support

Consider bringing a friend or supportive family member to the event. You can "retreat" to your friend for support. You can even get a bit of encouragement. You might say, "I just talked with the second person of five that I'm aiming for." Your friend says, "Good for you! Here, have a bite of this hors d'oeuvre."

Now, a bit refreshed, you take leave of your friend and step over to talk with a third person.

Or you could still feel some support by texting or calling a friend on your cell phone.

* * *

Many introverts find that they have different skills and positive tendencies than others (including extroverts).

A number of introverts are good listeners. Many are quite

thoughtful. Several introverts make others feel comfortable because they are listening and not battling for the limelight in the conversation.

Use the I.N.T.R.O. process:

I – Invest in building your energy

N – Nurture your lines before an event

T – Target reasonable goals

R – Recover as you go along

O – Organize support

Stop fighting any introvert tendencies you may have. Give yourself a break. Instead, support yourself and let go of berating yourself for being different from extroverts. Be sure to renew your personal energy.

There are extroverts longing to have a kind introvert listen to them.

You can be that supportive person.

Often you'll find that you're building a good, new connection.

How will you set up reasonable goals for your appearance at a networking event? How many good conversations are you aiming for? Five? Seven? How will you take breaks (the RECHARGE step of the *3 Rs of Relax Your Way Networking*)?

_____

_____

_____

_____

Relax Your Way Networking

For Introverts — Secrets to Excel #2

How Introverts Can Do Well When Others Want Them to "Talk Faster"

Some introverts say, "I don't like to meet new people at networking events because people are expecting me to respond quickly. Instead, I like to think through my responses."

One way an introvert can deal with this pressure to reply quickly is to say: "I've not thought of that quite that way before. I might need to pause for a moment. I want my response to be useful to our conversation."

For many of us, simply saying the above comment gives us more time to think of our next reply. Why? On average, people's brain tends to work at 700 words a minute, so your brain is already looking for your answer to a question. You are just giving it more time.

There is strategy involved with saying, "I might need to pause for a moment." You are letting the other person know what *you* are doing, and you're not asking the other person to do something.

Another alternative is the following form of response: "I

have two replies to your question."

"Yes?" asks the other person.

"I have my first impression, and then there's my reply that's based on my pausing and considering the details a bit longer. I prefer thinking about a question for a moment or two."

It is best to avoid using the above methods too much, but they *can* be used sparingly and well.

What comment do you want to express when someone presses you for a quick reaction to a topic? How will you get more time to think through your answer?

_____

_____

_____

_____

_____

_____

_____

_____

_____

For Introverts—Secrets to Excel #3

Special Note: Giving a speech provides you with a special advantage: Your credibility rises skyward. I know a number of speakers who self-identify as introverts. Still, they've learned to speak and create trust—and do well in business.

Introverts as Excellent Public Speakers

My leg shook like a hummingbird's wings while I played the piano for thirty-one seniors at a retirement home. As my little nine-year-old hands danced on the keyboard, I was terrified of making a mistake or having my shaking foot slip off the piano's sustain pedal. One slip and a big THUD sound would crash the piano recital.

About twenty years later, I stood up from my chair in the middle of an audience of 500 people and asked questions of the multi-millionaire speaker. The speaker gave me a pointed critique of my business card. I was learning, but then I noticed that my right leg was shaking violently. Oh!—it was back: my hummingbird-flutter leg.

Soon I sat down. I asked my girlfriend about how I did.

She said, "You did well." She had *not* noticed my shaking leg. This alerted me to the fact that on the inside one can be nervous, but *you can simultaneously look professional on the outside.*

This is an important distinction. Every year I help new speakers use methods to do well when giving a speech.

Introverts have additional challenges when it comes to giving a speech. To overcome such challenges, we will use the A.I.M. process:

A – Align with friendly faces
I – Increase one-to-one conversations
M – Make moments to "think through"

1. Align with friendly faces

Introduce yourself to audience members *before* your give your speech. Say, "Hi. I'm _____, and I'm you're speaker for today. I'm wondering if you came up with a question when you first learned of the title of today's speech. What topic, if I can address it, would really help you?" Take a few notes as the person talks, and ask for the person's name.

Meet around five people. Then when you are on stage, you will already have friendly faces in the audience. You can address these individuals and the process will be more like talking to one person at a time.

In fact, you can say, "Before this presentation, I was talking with a number of you, and Susan mentioned the XYZ project and how . . . "

This builds a better connection with the audience.

2. Increase one-to-one conversations

A number of introverts have told me, "I'm fine when talking to one person, but I'm thrown off when I speak to a group." My answer is: Approach your speech as a series of one-to-one conversations. Pick someone to talk with on the right side of the room, and pick one from the middle and one from the left side. The helpful phenomenon is that when you speak to one person, the people in front and behind that person feel like you're talking to them, too.

By the way, if anyone looks tired or distracted, simply shift your eyes to someone else. You are likely to find someone who resonates with your presentation. Talk to that person.

3. Make moments to "think through"

Introverts often feel extra pressure while they give a speech. Many say, "I don't like to give a hasty answer to someone's question. I prefer to think through a topic and then give a well-thought-out answer."

This makes sense since many introverts treasure alone time to do some research and find well-supported answers.

We will cover four methods so that you can think through your answer.

Method #1: Take a drink of water. While you have some water, you can think about the question and formulate your answer. (Also, reach for the water if your mind goes blank for a moment. The water buys you some time.)

Method #2: Say, "I'll need to pause for a moment. I want my answer to be useful to you."

Method #3: Say, "I haven't looked at it quite that way before. I'll need to pause for a moment. I want my answer to be helpful to you."

Method #4: Say, "I like to give thoughtful answers. So first, I'll give you an impression. And then I'll talk about what I find to be important considerations when we talk about _____. In fact, I'll suggest what a good solution would include..."

The above phrases help you have time to think through your answer. Memorize these phrases so you can easily say them. Simultaneously, your mind will work at 700 words a minute to find a good answer.

As an introvert, take advantage of your ability to think deeply. Just give yourself some more time.

Finally, here is an important observation. When you're speaking, a pause seems longer. But to the audience, a pause is not that long because they are thinking and trying to keep up with you. The material is all new to them. Or at least, they are learning about your point of view.

They want you to pause. They want to hear smart and thought-through details.

Good. As an introvert, you provide the clarity the audience craves.

When you provide clarity you are perceived as an expert, and it is easier to get more clients.

On what topic are you an expert? Inspired by a comment from Bob Bly, I came up with this phrasing: "Definition of an Expert: Someone who has created a system that people like and use." **So you do NOT need to know everything about a topic. If you have devised a system that works and people like using such a system, you will provide great value in your speech. List three potential topics here.**

_____

_____

_____

Protect and Build Your Energy #1

Special Note: To do well at a networking event you need a lot of personal energy. Some books only focus on techniques at an event. With *Relax Your Way Networking*, I'm interested in you as a whole person. So in this section, we will help you nurture yourself. Then you'll have an abundance of energy, and you will be more likely to let go of avoiding networking events. Additionally, you'll have positive energy that will create warm connections at the networking event.

How You Can Rescue Yourself from Feeling Overwhelmed

"I feel overwhelmed," my client, Serena, said.

"I can help you with that. We'll use two simple steps," I replied.

We'll use the D.O. process:

D – drop the nonessential

O – organize to "load share"

1. Drop the nonessential

If you feel overwhelmed, see if you can implement this strategy "load shed and load share."

We'll begin with "load shed."

When we feel overwhelmed, it's often when we're carrying too much of a burden. Along this line: One of the first things that Steve Jobs did on his return to Apple was cancel a number of projects.

"People think focus means saying yes to the thing you've got to focus on. But that's not what it means at all. It means saying no to the hundred other good ideas that there are. You have to pick carefully…. Innovation is saying no to 1,000 things." – Steve Jobs

While Walt Disney was leading The Walt Disney Company, he refused many outside projects. Roy O. Disney (Walt's brother and partner) explained the rationale for rejecting many projects: *"Decision-making is easy if your values are clear."*

So clarify your values. What do you personally stand for? If you're running a company, what is the company's mission?

We create energizing, encouraging edutainment for our good and humankind's rise.

– The Mission Statement of Tom Marcoux Media, LLC

You notice how brief my company's Mission Statement is. Brevity is important. For example, at a luncheon I attended, President Bill Clinton addressed the audience. He said, "If you can't say why you want to be President in one minute, then you don't know."

Similarly, I reduced my company's mission to 11 words.
Now it's your turn.

Answer these questions for yourself:

- What are my values?
- What can I drop from my current schedule that does *not* match my highest good?

2. Organize to "load share"

"I think one of my strengths is that I can always take advice, and I can delegate. I know a lot of people feel the need to do everything themselves, but I am not one of them."
– Dasha Zhukova

If you have not delegated some work in your life, then you have probably failed to empower people to do a good job.

We're not looking for perfection (that would be how you would do it); we're looking for good work that creates successful outcomes.

"Life is about success, not perfection." – Alan Weiss

I think of **three elements of delegation** in particular:

A – arrange a buffer
I – invest enough in training
M – measure the meaningful

Here are some brief insights:

A – arrange a buffer

If possible, make sure that the schedule has a buffer zone —so if the team member makes a mistake, the situation can be saved in time.

I – invest enough in training

People often fail because the team leader did not invest enough time and effort to make sure the person was adequately trained. Be sure to double-check that the person understands how to do a good job.

M – measure the meaningful

Team members often find their own way to accomplish the objective. Perhaps, you have a particular method in mind like making 21 cold calls a day. Then one team member innovates a plan to get people to call into your company. The person uses a targeted mailing list and a postcard that inspires appropriate people to call. Applaud the person's ingenuity! Your team members will likely find their own spin to the process. Measure what is important: Good results are good results.

"To delegate effectively, managers must recognize their own fears and allow some room for their team to make mistakes. With adequate development and trust, team members will more often meet the challenge than fail." – Robert Tanner

"No person will make a great business who wants to do it all himself or get all the credit." – Andrew Carnegie

If you're feeling overwhelmed, there are things you can do.

Remember: drop the nonessential and organize to "load share."

What are three nonessential things you can drop?

_____

_____

_____

Protect and Build Your Energy #2

Discover the Powerful Question that Helps You Attract Success

"I feel stuck," my friend Stephen said.

"I can help with that," I replied. We went further in our discussion until I found out that Stephen was ready for the question that could get him moving forward and doing better.

Here's the question:

What are you doing to keep yourself full of life?

To put it in few words, people are attracted to energy.

If you're dragging through your day, you need to take action to bring your tone back up.

"Better keep yourself clean and bright; you are the window through which you must see the world." – George Bernard Shaw

Earlier today, I had a delightful phone conversation—full of hope and energy.

How did that happen? I'm consistently reaching out to new people and seeking how I can be of service. Many times, I meet someone who does have a positive approach to life. In essence, we give each other the gift of good energy.

Discover the Power of Empowering Questions:
Author Randy Gage begins his day with a number of empowering questions.
I have adopted two of his questions in particular:
- What can I do today to be of service?
- Who do I know that needs a text, call, or card from me today?

I invite you to consider focusing on these questions and taking daily action related to them. Why? You will simply feel better because you will be "self-generating hope." By this I mean, if you can take action and brighten someone's day, you know deep in your heart that you are blessed; you do have power; you do make a difference.

"Happiness is not a goal, but a by-product."
– Eleanor Roosevelt

Some people get stuck in the "hamster treadmill" of more toys, more food, and more leisure activities.

If you go after happiness directly by trying to get more toys, more food and more leisure activities, you may be really disappointed.

Instead, see if you can really engage with life.

"I don't know what your destiny will be, but one thing I know: the only ones among you who will be really happy are those who will have sought and found how to serve." – Albert Schweitzer

When talking with my clients, I ask: "What do you do on a daily basis to keep yourself full of life?"
Some of the answers include:

- listen to energizing music
- devote 15 minutes to putting together a puzzle
- devote 20 minutes to my hobby
- playing with my pet
- calling a friend on the phone
- taking a walk
- prayer time/quiet time/meditation time
- hugging family members

I'll add:
- Do something that gives you some progress toward a big dream
- Listen to someone; hear them out; encourage them
- Be good to your body [enough sleep, exercise, nutrition]
- Find ways to laugh everyday [talking with friends, seeing something funny via YouTube or recorded video]

Consider this:
"The three grand essentials of happiness are: Something to do, someone to love, and something to hope for."
– Alexander Chalmers

I invite you to take daily steps related to the elements: something to do, someone to love and something to hope for.

When you take good care of yourself, your personal energy is positive and attractive.

You'll attract more opportunities.

**What are you doing to keep yourself full of life?
Is there something you want to add to your life?**

Protect and Build Your Energy #3

Use a Cure for Feeling Down — Power Up Your Courage and Happiness

Many years ago, I took my first tentative steps to become a professional speaker. One day, I was listening to an audio recording of the most successful speaker of the time. "What's the use?" I thought. I was nothing like this guy. He was tall, Caucasian and loud. I was average height, Asian, and ... well ... What was I?

I was afraid.

What was the source of my fear? — I was comparing myself to Mr. Top Speaker.

Then I had a thought: "He *can't* be everywhere."

That was a thought that countered my comparing myself to him and thinking that I could not compete with Mr. Top Speaker.

Yes, he could *not* be everywhere, and besides in the beginning, I would be speaking where he would *not* want to present, anyway. I took small steps forward ... and more opportunities arrived. (I've been a professional member of the National Speakers Association for more than 14 years.)

"Mr. Top Speaker" wasn't in the classroom teaching Stanford University MBA students ... I was.

He wasn't teaching a college level online Comparative Religion course (that I wrote) ... I was.

He wasn't writing the 31 books that I wrote.

My point is: You can quickly make yourself scared and actually put yourself into a dis-empowered mood by comparing yourself to someone further along than you are.

On the other hand ...

It you're feeling down, focus on this point:

Don't compare. DO Create.

By the way, comparing does not work because no one else can be You At Your Best.

To this day, there are plenty of people who still do not like Mr. Top Speaker. And there are a significant number of people who come up to me and express how they really relate to my speaking style and what I said in my speech.

Further, I'll share a secret. You do NOT need to create by yourself.

I've learned so much from mentors, books, colleagues and my graduate students—and my experiences with my clients.

The Cure for Feeling Down is: Create something.

Create something artistic.

Create a moment when someone smiles. You can simply say: "Hey, Susan, one thing I appreciate about you is ..." And then offer the person a sincere compliment.

Use the Power of G.A.G.

As a feature film director, actor and former stuntman, I know that a stunt is called a "gag"—in the film industry. I did a number of gags—including hanging on by my fingertips to the hood of a cherry-red 50's Chevy truck going 63 miles an hour. [I do not recommend this!]

I'm talking about the "gag" because I want you to remember a special G.A.G.

Do you feel low? Remember G.A.G.: "Gratitude, Action, Giving."

Gratitude – Ask yourself what am I grateful for? Write it down.

Action – Identify some simple, small action you can take to create progress for your dream.

Giving – Identify something you can do to help someone feel better. Then do it or at least get it into your day planner or calendar.

Let's say I go through some tough moments with a bitter, elderly relative. I find that my spirits go up when I help someone during my next phone call. Maybe I just listen intently. People appreciate being listened to. (I even wrote a book about this process titled, Be *Heard and Be Trusted*.) When you help someone else, you feel better.

"Happiness is a perfume you cannot pour on others without getting a few drops on yourself." – Ralph Waldo Emerson

The point is: When you are feeling grateful, this focus crowds out feeling down or inadequate.

As an Executive Coach, I help my clients identify the next actions to help them move toward their dream. My clients discover that taking action lifts their spirits in this present moment.

Remember: Don't compare; DO Create.

What can you create? You do not have to do the stereotypical creative things like writing and doing artwork. Coming up with a schedule that accommodates multiple family members is creative (for example).

_____

_____

_____

_____

_____

_____

_____

_____

_____

_____

_____

_____

Protect and Build Your Energy #4

Stop Holding Yourself Back—
The Hidden Truth for You to Rise to Big Success

"No, I can't get myself to get excited about a possible, positive thing," my friend Eldon said.

"I'm just curious. When did you last really look forward to something?" I asked.

"I don't know. Maybe sometime when I was a kid," he replied.

In working with hundreds of clients, graduate/college students and audience members, I've seen something insidious that causes big problems.

It centers on something connected to this question: Why do you hold back from affirming the positive?

Have you seen yourself afraid to hope?!

I have a vital question for you: 'Do you hold back from hoping for something because you hold some idea that you can*not* endure a big disappointment?

Here's the truth: *Even if you hide and try to play small, disappointments come into our lives, anyway!*

My solution is: **Until I know differently, I AM affirming the positive.**

Think about it: What if things do go your way? — then you would have *wasted your time* keeping yourself stuck in a negative spiral of thoughts.

The successful people I have interviewed have faced lots of disappointing outcomes and even rejection every week. How? They're always stretching and putting themselves out into the world.

Have you ever heard a friend say this: "Ahhh, what's the use? That kind of good thing never happens to me." And then the person does NOTHING. Beware of this terrible pattern of doing nothing.

"Nothing ventured, nothing gained." – Benjamin Franklin

Let's look at this evidence.

For many of us:
- There was the day when we could not ride a bicycle ... and then we did.
- There was the day that we had no job ... and then we had a first job.
- There was the day when we could not swim ... and then we could swim.

The truth is: *The past does not equal the future. – Tony Robbins*

However, if you do not hold a positive picture of your future, you are likely to do NOTHING! That's a big problem. And that is NOT for you.

So I invite you to consider using my method: **Until I know differently, I AM affirming the positive.**

As an Executive Coach and Spoken Word Strategist, I support my clients in boldly holding a positive picture of their future and taking consistent action.

Let's say you want to improve your skills and rise up the ladder and increase your hourly rate.

I know people who worked over years to improve their skills and to get excellent experience. They started at $5.00 per hour and now earn over $400 per hour.

This is doable when a person deeply wants to improve — and is willing to train hard.

"If you work hard on your job you can make a living, but if you work hard on yourself, you'll make a fortune" – Jim Rohn

One of my favorite sayings is: *"Replace worry with action" – Steve Chandler.*

Do NOT fall into the rut (or stay there) of those people who say that their lives are: "Same old, same old."

Do something new. Replace worry with action. Get some new learning. Learn from people who know things that you do not know.

As you do new things, keep up your own morale (and the morale of people near you).

How?

Until you know differently, Affirm the positive.

Yes – you're learning.

Yes – you're making progress for more abundance in your life.

Yes – you have a bright future—with advancements you do not even know about at the moment.

Yes – the project you're working on will have great outcomes (some of which you do not even know right now).

And here is the Hidden Truth: If you do meet a setback or a big disappointment, you CAN endure, bounce back and leap higher than before.

Why? Because by taking action you've learned so much more than others who do nothing, risk nothing and stay locked "in their shell" — or comfort zone.

Joy and success are outside your comfort zone.

Take action today.

Have you seen yourself afraid to hope? Write down three times that you have faced big disappointments but you still made it through okay. Do you see how you're made of strong stuff and can endure disappointment? Now you can move forward with possible action toward positive opportunities.

_____

_____

_____

_____

_____

_____

_____

_____

_____

Protect and Build Your Energy #5

Keep Making Your Life Better! — The Blessing of Wayne Dyer's Wisdom

"There is no way to happiness, happiness is the way," said Dr. Wayne Dyer. In these days, since Wayne Dyer passed away, I'm thinking about those brief, life-enhancing quotes he gave us.

Let's see how these three pithy quotes inspire our empowering patterns of thought now.

1. "There is no way to happiness, happiness is the way." – Wayne Dyer

How much ice cream will make you happy? How many new cars?

People who get caught up in the "hamster treadmill" of trying to go directly to happiness through more toys, more food and more experiences may find themselves greatly disappointed.

If that's true, then where is happiness? Happiness is in this moment – doing what you are now doing.

There are plenty of ways to get caught up in what makes us miserable. One pervasive way is to get stuck in worrying.

"Replace worry with action." – Steve Chandler

So I invite you to use this empowering pattern. When a worrisome thought arises, think "Stop—Replace."

I've found this to be helpful because in running my own company, I've had moments of serious worry. Then I remember "Replace worry with action."

Other times, I have a thought, "Oh! I have so much to do."

Then I tell myself: "STOP." And I replace the thought with:

"I am doing this one thing in this one moment. I'll do the next thing after this one thing."

So in the spirit of Wayne's comment "There is no way to happiness, happiness is the way":

Seek to make the way you're living moment to moment into a "happy path." You deep breathe. You connect with feeling gratitude for the blessings you do have in this moment.

2. "If you change the way you look at things, the things you look at change." – Wayne Dyer

Think of the reflexive way we look at things:
- "That will make me happy."
- "That's going to hurt."
- "You're wrong. And you hurt me."

Certainly, we do not look at everything as if it will hurt us. Still, we spend a lot of time judging people and things.

Think about it. Are you using your brain in a skillful manner?

Every time a worrisome thought arises, do you obsess over it?

Wayne's comment: "If you change the way you look at things, the things you look at change" inspires us to find new, empowering ways to interpret our life situation.

When a pain-inducing thought arises, consider these new ways to look at your current situation:
- What can I learn here?
- What lesson would Higher Power have me learn so I can make my life better and better?

3. "There is no scarcity of opportunity to make a living at what you love; there's only scarcity of resolve to make it happen." – Wayne Dyer

Some people will hold onto the idea that Wayne Dyer was just one of the "lucky ones."

But let's remember, he faced a big risk earlier in life. Wayne left his tenured teaching position at St. John's University in New York to pursue his destiny as both speaker and author. Yes—it worked for him.

This statement "There is no scarcity of opportunity to make a living at what you love; there's only scarcity of resolve to make it happen" is a big challenge to many of us. Really?—you can make a living at what you love?

I have an answer to this question. I say, "Let's find out!"

At different times in my life, I've made a living doing what felt personally meaningful to me. I've earned income as a graduate school instructor, as a model/actor (years ago), as a speaker, and as an author. Now, I do a lot of work as an Executive Coach and Spoken Word Strategist.

Are there times when we need to do both a "rent job" and our "dream job"—simultaneously? Yes—I've seen that to be true. Many years ago, I worked at a bank for 8 hours a day and then raced home to edit a feature film for several hours—everyday! Thank goodness, I had a great friend to help me edit the feature film.

If you love writing poetry, perhaps, you may not make a living at it. Still, let's look again at Wayne's phrase: "There is no scarcity of opportunity." For some poets, they might find an opportunity to earn income by setting their poetry to music—in song writing.

I'll emphasize that Wayne invites us to have the resolve to make it happen. Will it be your destiny to make a large income at what you love doing? Who knows?

Still, what we can know is: You will not find out unless you resolve to persist and keep taking effective action.

Wayne said, "You can never get enough of what you don't want."

I've seen people get stuck in "golden shackles." They do a job they hate and then give themselves the salve of big, expensive vacations. They say, "I deserve this."

Wayne's comment, "You can never get enough of what you don't want" relates to how you can*not* fill the hole of a job you hate with enough vacations or toys (cars, etc.).

Wayne said that when he was drinking to excess that he *could never get enough alcohol-laden drinks*. Because he did NOT want the alcohol.

He wanted a better life.

I invite you to reflect on Wayne's above quotes and see how you might step up your actions for your own better life.

What would constitute a better life for you?

_____

_____

_____

Protect and Build Your Energy #6

Live Fearlessly

"I feel stuck," my friend Kathy said. "I can help with that," I replied. During our discussion, I asked, "So how are you with fear in your life?"

Stuck and fear are related.

As an Executive Coach and Spoken Word Strategist, I help clients frequently rise above fear. We use the C.A.N. process.

C – change the frame
A – assess your "Fearless-Action"
N – nurture yourself

1. Change the frame

How does fear paralyze us? It controls how we "frame a situation" — in other words, how we *perceive* a situation.

If we see a situation with "the eyes of fear" our vision is *restricted.*

Worse than that, we cannot see ourselves adapting and succeeding during a crucial event or moment.

I've seen people fail to return a phone call or even send a resume due to personal fear.

It helps to consciously reframe one's thoughts and point of view.

For example, when I first aimed to get speaking engagements (some years ago), I was afraid of not having the "perfect" video, articles and supporting material in my speaker's kit.

Then I learned to transform my view of the situation from "they rejected me" or "they will reject me" to *a new frame* of "We did not have a match" and "It is all good practice."

This process is also known as "reframing."

How do you live fearlessly? You "fear" less.

By this I mean: "Turn down the volume on fear."

I'm often traveling in a car with a team member on my way to give a speech.

My team member likes to have music playing on the radio.

Often, I have moments in which I turn down the radio volume.

This is a good metaphor. In life, **I turn down the fear and turn UP the rehearsal.**

So in the car, I turn down radio volume and rehearse for my upcoming speech.

Instead of ruminating over my fear of making any error in speaking, I fill up my thoughts and consciousness with excellent rehearsal.

I give fear LESS space in my conscious mind.

Now it's your turn.

How can you turn down the volume of your personal fear? How can you rehearse or prepare—and focus on that process of making yourself ready and capable of excellent performance?

2. Assess your "Fearless-Action"

Ask yourself: "What would I do if I was not stopped by fear?"

Early in my business career, I found myself failing to ask for referrals.

Then I learned to query myself with: **"What would I do if I was not stopped by fear?"**

The answer was: "I'd ask for a referral."

So I discovered something useful: I could **assess what would be my "Fearless-Action."** This is the action I would take if fear were absent.

[This became part of my program "Get Clients Fearlessly."]

Now it's your turn.

What would you do—perhaps, a small action—if fear was not present nor was it holding you back? How can you take a small action in the fearless direction?

3. Nurture yourself

To act in a fearless (or *"not encumbered by fear"*) manner, you need lots of personal energy. To stretch in your life, takes energy and strength.

Imagine how many times we fail to take the courageous action because "I'm so tired" or "I don't feel strong enough." We may feel that we're too tired to be able to "think on our feet."

Much of the process for creating more success in our lives requires quick adapting and thinking on one's feet.

I speak often in front of groups—so I rehearse often.

In fact, before every networking event I practice my answer to this question: "Tom, what do you do?"

My answer is: "I help people create High Trust Relationships so they gain more success and the Golden Yes."

I remember the first time I asked for a fee of $400 per hour. To deal with any fear, I rehearsed saying that amount firmly and smoothly. Was I scared? Sure. Was I well-rehearsed? YES.

More than that, I made sure to take a walk and relax before I placed the important phone call.

Be sure to nurture yourself.

I remember attending a special event and listening to author Zig Ziglar saying: "If you had a thoroughbred racehorse, would you feed him junk food and deny him sleep? Of course not. You would take good care of him!"

Yes—let's treat ourselves at least as well as a horse!

Now it's your turn.

How can you nurture yourself and build up a reserve of personal energy?

* * *

To live fearlessly means that you consciously work to "fear" less.

Quiet down fear. Turn the fear volume down.

Do not wait for the absence of fear.

Instead, fill your mind with empowering thoughts, plans and action.

We can use fear as a signal for more preparation and rehearsal.

That's useful.

Beyond that, fill your life with action and aiming for what you truly want.

"Courage is not the absence of fear but rather the judgment that something is more important than fear." – Meg Cabot

You can enjoy more moments of the day focused on progress and moving forward.

How can you build up your personal energy? Then you'll be more likely to avoid giving into fear.

_____

_____

_____

_____

_____

_____

_____

_____

Tom Marcoux

Protect and Build Your Energy #7

Courage and How You'll Succeed and Feel Happy

"What do you mean 'It takes courage to be happy'?" my client Maria asked.

"You need the courage to say 'I am happy' each day. Because only you will declare it and make it manifest in your life," I replied. I know this to be a fact. How? I have friends who merely complain about things that didn't turn out the way they prefer. On the other hand, the most successful people I know appreciate all of the blessings in their life. We'll use the I. A.M. process:

I – inquire

A – aim for joy

M – make space in your day

When you say, "I am", you are programming yourself. This is important. ***Your power manifests in your own choice of your programming.***

1. Inquire

Ask yourself, "Why am I happy?"

You might ask, "How does this question help?"

The reason is that without the question, many of us will fail to see what is good and enjoyable in this moment.

Ask these questions:
- Why am I happy in this moment?
- What is happiness for me?
- Why am I content?

If you're going through a really tough time, it is hard to focus on happiness.

I can relate. When my elderly mother was in the hospital (some time ago) for an extended stay, I was quite concerned. And, *I was grateful* that my sweetheart was there supporting me through the daily extended visits.

As an Executive Coach, I help people make a shift in focus so they do the next action—one that is powerful and positive. Often to take the next and positive action, it really helps to *ask an empowering question.*

So try these helpful questions:
- What am I grateful for—in this moment?
- What is still going well in other parts of my life?

My own personal coach asked me, "Tom, why are you happy?" I immediately replied, "Because I know who I am. And what I want. And what direction I am going in."

You may notice that my happiness did not rest on getting any one thing at any particular time. I remember this quote:

"Happiness is not a goal; it is a by-product."

– Eleanor Roosevelt

I would add: **"You'll find happy moments when you're going in the direction of your highest good. A lot of happy moments arise in the context of expressing love, creativity and contribution to humankind's rise."**

2. Aim for joy

If you do not make enjoying your journey of life as one of your priorities, you'll miss it.

For example, one of my friends insists that life is merely a test and happiness only exists in the afterlife. And guess what? She is the most miserable and sickliest person I know.

Researchers talk about the "self-fulfilling prophesy" and how our thoughts manifest in our moods and physical health. In fact, there are decades of research in the field of psychoneuroimmunology that support this viewpoint.

My point is that I find the people, with more energy and doing kind things and great achievements, are generally happy about what they're doing in life.

By the way "aim for joy" does not mean you'll avoid disappointments. In fact, when you have specific goals you may experience "more disappointments." However, you'll have the energy to bounce back faster. It's worth it. Life goes up and down, and with bumpy times—and that's better than a flat, "blaaaaah" approach to life.

3. Make space in your day

So how busy are you? Whoa! **Wrong question.**

How about: "What do you regret failing to place into your daily life?"

The truth is: we're all too busy, and life slams us with demands each day.

Now what?

Well, you could remain like a puppy on a raft in the middle of the ocean, buffeted around by the currents.

Or you could gain or build a motor and guide your raft forward in the direction you choose.

My point is that everyday I make time for laughter and creativity and time with my sweetheart and friends (at least on the phone). Since I developed these habits I have (for many years) enjoyed wonderful amounts of energy and excellent health.

When I talk about making space in your day, I'm including *"writing a second draft"* of something you would say to someone else [or yourself].

For example, recently, I was in the restroom, and I saw that a family member had left an empty toilet tissue roll.

My first thought was to say to the family member, "Apparently, you don't remember the episode of the TV Show *Mad About You* when the Helen Hunt-character taught her husband to change the toilet paper roll."

Now if I actually said that, what do you think I would have received? At minimum, a dirty look. Perhaps, 30 minutes of arguing. Instead, I *avoided* saying any type of sarcastic remark, and the evening turned out warm and joyful.

So now, I'm asking you to *pause before you say the first thought that pops up in your mind* like a knee-jerk reaction. **"Write a second draft" and seek to speak positive words to your friends and loved ones.** That is, make space in your day for happiness.

I invite you to be courageous and declare "I am happy" and find your daily answers to: "Why am I happy in this moment?" You'll be different. And you may need to keep your answers (to "Why am I happy in this moment?") mostly private. Why? Some people are not happy and they do not want to hear about someone doing well. Be sure to limit your time with such people. **When you're happy, you spread happiness.**

How can you make space in your day for happy moments?

Protect and Build Your Energy #8

How to Really Nurture Yourself and Expand Your Success and Happiness

"I don't know how to do it. How do I ever forgive myself?" my family member asked.

"That's a big conversation. It might take many conversations. I want you to know that I believe in my heart that you did the best you could do with what you knew at the time," I replied.

Much is made of the idea of compassion and self-compassion.

Still, many of us were trained that feeling guilty and angry at ourselves is the special way to "push ourselves to be good people."

Years ago, I came across a phrase that has remained in my thoughts for decades.

"To love is to be happy with." – Barry Neil Kaufman

We notice that this phrase is NOT "to love is to beat up, make feel awful, to shame, and to push around until a person feels like garbage."

My father threw me into walls. That was not love.

I'm grateful that I had loving mentors later in life.

I had three high school instructors who demonstrated compassion, kindness and coaching to me:

One taught me psychology—I earned a degree in psychology.

One taught me English literature—I wrote 31 books, screenplays—and I directed feature films.

One taught me theology—I wrote a college level, online Comparative Religion course that I teach—for over 14 years.

So I learned compassion somewhere else than from my father.

How to Really Nurture Yourself

Here's something helpful: Have a simple principle to get to the compassionate action.

Ask yourself this question: "How would I act toward a good friend?"

Treat yourself as you would treat a good friend.

That, in a way, is a shortcut to caring for yourself in a self-compassionate manner.

Would you help your friend by giving him or her a good meal, time for appropriate sleep, time for fun and enjoyment? Of course, you would.

If your friend made a mistake, would you assault his or her ears with nonstop berating. No!

"If you want others to be happy, practice compassion.
If you want to be happy, practice compassion."
– The Dalai Lama

Let's return to this phrase:

"To love is to be happy with." – Barry Neil Kaufman

I suggest that self-compassion can help you step forward to improved success and happiness. Part of my reasoning is that practicing self-compassion gives you more positive energy. Such energy will help you attract more opportunities.

Fear brings about much negative energy. Here's a specific example. My sweetheart has crossed the line beyond "being on the heavy side" to being severely overweight and unhealthy. I fear that she'll cross the line and fall into diabetes (like her mother endures).

My approach is to quiet down my fear and to support her. I do this by going on a walk with her every day. We often walk 8,000 to 10,000 steps.

Drop the habits of fear and of using guilt to push anyone. Be kind. Be supportive.

My point is: Be kind to yourself and enhance and expand your positive energy. Take that energy and apply it to serving others and expand your prosperity, too.

How can nurture yourself? What specific actions will you do to bring more happy moments into your daily life?

_____

_____

_____

_____

Tom Marcoux

Protect and Build Your Energy #9

How You Can Get Beyond Fear— to Your Best Life!

"I'm afraid that . . ."—and a number of people stop the conversation right there. Instead, I take the acknowledgement of fear as just the beginning of the conversation. I'm not looking to ignore fear. I'm looking to quiet it down and get on with the joy and success of each day.

That's what we're here to talk about. **You can master fear so you can create the life you love.**

Otherwise, you're stuck in this mess:
- Fear acts as a success inhibitor.
- Fear acts as a love inhibitor.
- Fear acts as a patience inhibitor.

For many people, we can observe that fear is the springboard of greed.

It's like they get stuck in "Don't touch my stuff!—there's not enough to go around!"

Do NOT let fear inhibit you from taking positive action.

Instead use fear in a skillful manner. How? Use it as an invitation for awareness and as a stepping stone for you to take intelligent, positive and courageous action.

You CAN convert fear into "get prepared-energy." Rehearse.

As an Executive Coach and Spoken Word Strategist, I help my clients use strategy in how they speak and rehearse so they bring ease to tough situations like giving a speech or leading a vital meeting.

We'll use the C.A.N. process:

C – care that fear is there
A – align with courage
N – nurture yourself

1. Care that fear is there

Let's acknowledge what we fear.

One time my sweetheart saw that I was talking faster and my face had a frantic expression.

"What are you afraid of?" she asked me. I said, "I'm afraid that the get-together will not go well and that I'll lose the goodwill of my colleague."

Just as I said that, I had a new thought. "Okay. If it is a 'disaster,' how can I make it still something positive?" That opened a new line of thinking. I said, "If no one is there, *I'm* there and *my colleague* is there. I'll serve my colleague. We'll do a coaching session and I'll still make it worth her time."

My point is: Yes! Go ahead think it through. What is the worst case scenario?

Ask yourself these questions:

- How can I still make sure there is less damage?
- How can I conduct my own actions in a

trustworthy and respectful manner?
- What will I learn here?
- Will I have stepped out and shown the world I am able to do good work at the level I'm at now?

Write up a detailed plan that uses the above questions as a springboard for you to do well even if things don't go the way you prefer.

2. Align with courage

Ever see the face of someone who says, "I don't like rollercoasters" but the person has a Big Smile, after the person has ridden a rollercoaster?

Why the smile? Because he or she survived!

Years ago, I really did not like rollercoasters—in particular the wooden ones that slam you about.

In Las Vegas, Nevada (at New York–New York Hotel and Casino), I held my sweetheart's hand and we slooowly went up the hill before the rollercoaster plummets down the first dip.

I turned to her and said, "No matter what happens, know that I love you."

She laughed.

Okay—it was comedic opportunity and I seized the moment.

Still, I knew that she likes rollercoasters and I was going to ride other rollercoasters with her—in the future.

So I decided to change my approach and perception of rollercoasters.

"Courage is not the absence of fear but rather the judgment that something is more important than fear." – Meg Cabot

3. Nurture yourself

To face fear, you need something in particular: your personal energy. I've learned that pain and fear drain energy from us. So we need to nurture ourselves so we have the energy to rehearse, study and/or receive coaching.

As an Executive Coach, I help clients to schedule in rehearsal and appropriate breaks and renewal time.

We can look at this analogy that I first heard from author Zig Ziglar. If you have a thoroughbred horse, you won't feed him junk food. And you will walk the horse after a race to cool the horse down.

We take good care of horses, dogs and cats.

Let's be sure that you nurture yourself.

It's tougher to be courageous, if you're feeling run down.

Do *not* let that happen! Take good care of yourself so you have an abundance of personal energy.

Take notes. Observe yourself. What brings your energy back to a high level?

For example, in just a few moments from now, I'll be reading one of my stories in my upcoming collection of fiction to a good friend of mine.

We'll have so much fun talking about the science fiction details!

Take good care of yourself, and then you can move beyond fear into your full, positive potential.

Now it's your turn.

What is more important to you than fear? Will you get coaching and do some rehearsal?

Write your answers to these questions:
- How can I still make sure there is less damage?
- How can I conduct my own actions in a trustworthy and respectful manner?

- What will I learn here?
- Will I have stepped out and shown the world I am able to do good work at the level I'm at now?

Tom Marcoux

Protect and Build Your Energy #10

How to Keep Your Heart Full and Keep Moving Forward

"Damn! He did it again," my friend Nadine said. Her husband had promised to pick up the dry cleaning but had failed to do so.

I know at times, we need to rely on others. But sometimes, we'll get significantly disappointed.

Recently I wrote: **"Collaboration, friendliness and kindness combine as a terrific form of power."** So I'm aware of the how great things can go when people come together. I'm currently leading teams in the United Kingdom, India and the United States of America—so teams mean a lot to me.

Still, my question is: *How do you keep your heart full?*

And that's related to this vital question: *Where is your hope coming from?*

Find some way to take personal action so that's the springboard for your hope.

If you're relying only on a human being to bring you hope, that may be a significant problem.

Human beings make errors, get distracted and put themselves first (at times) before others. Human beings, at times, break promises.

How about keeping a promise to yourself—to keep growing, discovering and learning?

I call this "self-generating hope."

There's another type of hope: "**Self**-generating hope." That's referencing your Higher **Self.**

Think of your Higher Self as that part of you that is connected with the Divine and with all the good in the universe. When you act from your Higher Self, you act with courage, and you're divinely guided.

The opposite is to act from your ego—that part of you that's made of fear.

We can tie this into "Where is your hope coming from?"

Don't wish it was easier, wish you were better. Don't wish for less problems, wish for more skills. Don't wish for less challenge, wish for more wisdom. – Jim Rohn

A powerful and healthy way to approach life is: *My hope arises from my Higher Self and from my taking action—positively and consistently.*

We can call this a proactive hope—a courageous hope.

The opposite would be a "wishy-washy hope." But that is NOT for you.

My friend, step forward. Keep nurturing yourself. Take action and exercise your Courageous Hope.

That's how you keep your heart full and you keep moving forward.

What is important to you? Consider this philosophy: *My hope arises from my Higher Self and from my taking action—positively and consistently.* **Does this appeal to you? Will you use it? How?**

_____

_____

_____

_____

_____

_____

_____

_____

_____

_____

Protect and Build Your Energy #11

Special Note: I'm including this section because to be at your best in a networking event, you need to take action so that you're not frazzled by what's going on in the office before the event.

Save Time — Lead Effectively — Increase Your Success (Time Affluence)

What is a springboard for your career success? Your ability to appear and even feel calm during crises provides you with the "great leader aura." You impress people. Then they look to you for leadership, and you achieve better and better results.

"Time Affluence" is essentially your moment-to-moment experience of feeling calm and in control. The opposite would be feeling overwhelmed and feeling everything is pushing on you at the same time.

When you are in the state of being, Time Affluent, your leadership is enhanced. People naturally cooperate with you!

Here are three big mistakes to avoid (which block the

experience of Time Affluence):

#1: Speaking in "Loser Language"
#2: Losing time to miscommunication and confusion
#3: Failing to Nurture "Catapult-Moments"

Mistake #1: Speaking in "Loser Language"
Yes, I used the term Loser Language to get your attention.

Right this minute, realize you are "on-stage" more than you know. You might think that you could say a casual comment, but you could be torpedoing your effectiveness.

Loser Language refers to seemingly innocent comments that make you appear unprofessional or even distraught.

A simple comment like: "Oh—it's all happening at the same time!" takes away from your perceived effectiveness as a leader.

It's better to develop your Calm-Control Language of an Effective Leader.

This is about the difference between Calm-Control Language versus Loser Language.

Calm-Control Language
 (versus Loser Language)

* We got this! One step at a time.
 (versus "It's all happening at the same time!")

* We can handle this situation.
 (versus "Damn! Another crisis!")

A leader who gets stuck in complaining or talking like he or she is frantic is losing points with subordinates and others like the Board Members.

Why is your language so important? The reason is that people follow so easily. Say a trigger word like "crisis" or "another damn problem" and people follow along and start commiserating, and positive energy flees the room.

Instead, you need to cultivate your own calm. Richard Carlson, author of *Don't Sweat the Small Stuff*, told me that he learned this idea: "Stop talking about how you're overwhelmed with too much to do. Instead, say "I'm doing one thing after another." Richard explained that he felt overwhelmed by a packed schedule of promoting one of his books. He was scheduled for 12 cities in 10 days for many appearances. But the truth was: Richard was only going to go to one city and appear One At A Time.

Why does this matter? Because we can all handle one thing at a time that follows another thing.

Instead of compounding the pain by thinking that "it's all happening at the same time!"—break it apart and look at one thing after another thing.

Develop the Mindset of Time Affluence. Focus on doing the next action (the best one for you).

Avoid the Mindset of complaining about too much to do and being overwhelmed. Merely using the language of "feeling overwhelmed" changes our experience of our present moment. Be careful. People can see your upset on your face.

Choose how you relate to your present moment.

You can be Time Affluent right now. How? Focus! Pick one thing to focus on—this is the one thing you are doing.

As an Executive Coach, I help clients focus on priorities and "droppables." One time I had 14 projects on my company's board. I dropped six projects, finished four fast and postponed other projects. Then I was down to four projects. That was better and smarter.

Too many projects dissipate energy and make us feel overwhelmed. STOP THAT.

When Steve Jobs returned to Apple, he canceled many projects. Jobs knew that focus is important to gain better results faster.

As a Vice-President or CEO (or just having a full-life of work and family), you may have a number of projects that company objectives require. However, you have control of your calendar. You can designate that the afternoon is focused on three projects (in their time slots).

The point here is: Have mental discipline to corral your focus. Make space to focus on doing one thing at a time. And focus on the idea that you can be Time Affluent. [I wrote a whole book on doing well with time: *Power Time Management: More Time, Less Stress, and Zero Procrastination (Your Breakthrough for More Success, Happiness and Time Off).*]

Solution #1: Guard your language.

Avoid being sloppy with your language. People are listening. Use neutral words like "handle this situation." You can say something like: "There are some tough elements of this situation, but we're good at this. We can handle this."

One leader used this focus point: "Rise above this." When anything went wrong, for example, certain supplies did not arrive for a presentation, he'd say, "Rise above this," and his team would find a solution.

One of my favorite examples is how Mark Burnett and his crew of the TV show *Survivor* solved the problem of needing to film on a remote island with no facilities for lodging or a production headquarters. Crew members said, "That's it. We can't do this."

Mark said, "We are doing this. I need to hear ideas." Soon

after, a team member suggested, "We could rent a cruise ship. It's like a floating city." They used a small speed boat to go from the cruise ship to shore.

This solution worked!

* * *

Mistake #2: Losing time to miscommunication and confusion

As an Executive Coach, I help the client see the whole picture.

In some cases, a leader defaults to a "run over people" manner OR the leader "does not lead strongly enough." Both of these default-settings need to be jettisoned.

Here is the powerful method to avoid miscommunication and confusion:

Solution #2: Use "Headlines" and "Taglines"

An effective leader gives the "headline" like: "I'm now going to talk about three possible solutions to the XY situation."

Then, the leader shows that she or he is open to input by using a tagline like this: "After I discuss the three possible solutions, I'm going to open this up. I want to hear your ideas, thoughts and feelings."

How do you eliminate miscommunication and confusion?

When you express a headline, the listener understands your point up front.

When you use a tagline, the listener feels comfortable and primed to offer useful ideas for the discussion.

Without effective leadership, team members often become

confused or distracted. For example, earlier I mentioned that you're on-stage more than you think. If you always walk past certain cubicles, then the team may think you're favoring the individuals in those cubicles.

My point here is: To protect your team from some individuals starting petty political maneuvers, pay close attention to what you're communicating.

* * *

Mistake #3: Failing to Nurture "Catapult-Moments"

When you do what's necessary to strengthen yourself, you can have Catapult-Moments. The catapult on an aircraft carrier kicks the plane Forward Fast. (My term *Catapult-Moment* is one of my favorites.)

As an Executive Coach, I work with clients so they develop skills, strength and stamina. Then the Catapult-Moments arise. You jump forward. You find something new and better. You experience extraordinary progress. Clarity arrives and you feel so alive!

I use a number of questions and patterns to help the person find their personalized Next Leap Upwards. That Next Leap Upwards is a Catapult-Moment. In my coaching, my clients experience the power of "insight-intuition-action" which create Catapult-Moments.

The effective leaders have their eyes wide-open for Catapult-Moments for the people who report to them.

Often, the leader facilitates the Catapult-Moment in a subordinate by asking questions like:
- What went right with Project XY?
- What didn't perform with Project XY?
- Do you need to do damage-control? How?
- Knowing what you know now, what would you do

differently for the next project?

The Important Point is: If you don't take good care of yourself, you may not have the personal stamina to stay alert for potential Catapult-Moments. Also, nurturing yourself will help you to have more patience with your team members who may have a slower speaking style or even a slower thinking style than your own.

As a CEO, I lead teams in multiple countries including the United Kingdom, India and the USA. Just like I learned as a feature film director, you direct each individual in a different way. That's why we stay alert to opportunities to foster your team members' Catapult-Moments.

Solution #3: Support your own well-being.

Use your notepad or personal journal, and answer these questions for yourself:

- What would be a Leap Upwards for your better life?
- What is one small step in the right direction?
- How can you make incremental progress that builds energy in you?

Remember, an effective leader is, in the first place, an effective leader of his or her own behavior and well-being. Monitor the essentials: Your exercise, sleep, nutrition and the results you achieve each week. Consider hiring an Executive Coach, so you raise your game.

* * *

To truly experience being Time Affluent, you guard your time by avoiding the 3 Big Mistakes:

#1: Speaking in "Loser Language"
#2: Losing time to miscommunication and confusion
#3: Failing to Nurture "Catapult-Moments"

Take strategic action.
The best to you.

What do you want most? Would it help for you to improve your habitual comments (and avoid "Loser Language")? How will you nurture "Catapult-Moments"?

_____

_____

_____

_____

_____

_____

_____

_____

_____

_____

Protect and Build Your Energy #12

"You Will Achieve More Than You Believe"

"What do you do as an Executive Coach?" Sheryl, a new acquaintance, asked me.

"I transform lives," I began. "When someone works with me, I let them know: *"You will achieve more than you believe."*

Then I continue, "I know this to be a **fact** because I had three great high school instructors:

One taught me psychology so I got a degree in psychology.

One taught me English literature so I wrote 31 books, screenplays—and I directed feature films.

One taught me theology and I wrote an online college level course in Comparative Religion that I've been teaching for over 14 years.

So I know: "You will achieve more than you believe."

By this I mean, these three instructors got me to think on an *expansive level*. I started to do things *beyond* my first level of belief.

In a past moment, you may have believed that you're

stuck.

You are NOT stuck. You can act in a way to take yourself to a higher level.

Once, while coaching a particular client, I said, "Stop telling the story of 'I'm indecisive.'"

I continued, "Instead, consider the story: 'I make decisions as they come up.'"

I invited this client to focus on the "verb" she wanted as in "I decide." And I invited her to drop the disempowering label of "indecisive."

So you can achieve more in the next moments of your life . . . we'll use the A.I.M. process:

A – arrange coaching
I – intensify rehearsal
M – make the hard decisions backed by action

1. Arrange coaching

Before I coach someone, I often send a customized list of questions via email before the new client's first session.

Here is an example:

1. What is the most important problem (detail) you're concerned about?

2. What one thing, when we handle it, would feel like we've really accomplished what you needed from the coaching sessions with me?

3. How can I help you most to make your work excellent?

4. What are you expecting or hoping in these coaching sessions?

5. In [the workshop when we worked together], what particularly worked for you?

6. Is there something you're particularly fearful about [with your project]? Give some details, please.

7. What is your ideal outcome for your [project]? What is the "pie-in-the-sky" positive result you would be thrilled with?

I coach in a unique way. I function as coach, consultant and mentor. I may say, "I'm now switching hats. I'm putting on my mentor hat."

I encourage the client to say Y.E.S. to his or her new life of higher levels of success and happiness:

Y – yearn for added knowledge
E – engage new systems and measurement
S – select criteria for excellence

I'll share a brief insight for each element.

Yearn for added knowledge
You do as well as you can with what you know at the time. When you know new methods, you can take different action.

Engage new systems and measurement
Knowledge is NOT enough. You need to measure the amount of new action you're taking. A *system* helps you naturally integrate the new method into your life.

Select criteria for excellence
Many people get stuck because they're trying to appear "perfect." Instead, *select criteria for excellence.* By this I mean, identify what must be in a project and what you can let go or drop from the endeavor.

2. Intensify rehearsal

Through rehearsal, you CAN do things that you've never done before.

My clients have rehearsed and then—
- directed a film
- given a speech in front of 157 people
- performed well in a job interview and gained a highly sought after job

I've learned that *Rehearsal is the answer to fear.*

3. Make the hard decisions backed by action

Make the decision to integrate a *new system* so you get new actions completed *consistently*.

Intensify systems

Instead of setting a tough goal and gritting your teeth and hoping to stay on your vigorous schedule, place a new system into your life. That is, a system for taking action that becomes a natural part of your day.

For example: recently, a colleague asked me to help her make sure that she rehearses enough for her next presentation.

I asked, "What do you do everyday?"

"Brush my teeth," she replied.

"How about rehearsing your speech for 3 minutes immediately before you complete brushing your teeth?" I suggested.

"I could do that," she replied.

Then I suggested that she set up a reward for herself when she completes three sessions of rehearsal.

Now, she had an *empowering system* of both specific actions and rewards.

Now it's your turn.

What do you want to make sure that you do on a daily basis? How can you reward yourself for taking action?

Measure the empowering way

Some people find it too painful to endure the emotional roller-coaster of weighing themselves everyday. A solution is to check one's weight only once a week.

Still, we do well when we focus on three important details about measuring: a) what, b) when, and c) meaning

For example, when I wanted to drop weight, I had these details:

1) What? What is my belt measurement? (I was glad when I had slimmed down to three notches slimmer on the belt.)

2) When? I programmed weighing myself once a week.

3) Meaning: The belt measurement was more important to me than the weight number because I was also doing weight training. Weight training builds muscle, and muscle fibers weigh more than fat or other tissues. So, for me, the weight number was NOT the only meaningful measurement

Vital Actions that Increase Your Leverage

Make the hard decision to find out what forms of leverage would make you more attractive to big opportunities. In business, to gain leverage, focus on these 3 *Golden Points of Leverage:*

1) your network (your contacts . . . How many people are in your esubscribers list, connected to you via LinkedIn.com, Twitter, Facebook?)

2) you have special knowledge (you're an expert; perhaps, you know current marketing trends)

3) you have access to target markets.

If you want someone to invest in your project or even choose your manuscript to publish, it really helps to express how you have the above *3 Golden Points of Leverage.*

What hard decisions do you face? What new action do you need to *systematize* into your life? Will you get coaching? What will be your schedule of rehearsal?

_____

_____

_____

_____

_____

_____

_____

_____

Protect and Build Your Energy #13

Through Action You Can Defy Past, Disempowering Labels

Do you call yourself a label that actually hurts you? Some people call themselves shy and then live like a shy person.

I have met several people who say, "I was shy when I was a child," and it's surprising because the "formerly shy person" now is a professional speaker.

When I was a child, I *acted* in shy ways.

Now, every week, I *act in courageous ways.*

I invite you to defy past, disempowering labels.

Those labels become obsolete when you act in a courageous way.

The problem is that we've been conditioned to categorize everything, including ourselves, quickly.

I have a family member who held, for years, to labeling herself "a depressed person." She believed it and acted like it.

Later, she adopted the idea of "I deal with depression symptoms." This was a fresh and empowering way to view her situation. In a number of ways, this idea "dealing with depression symptoms" gave her more freedom.

In any moment, she could act as a "courageous soul."

For example, if she had remained with the label "depressed person," she would have limited her behaviors. In her thoughts, a depressed person would not join Toastmasters and learn how to speak in front of a group. A depressed person would not have the energy. A depressed person would not have the strength to face fear and learn new skills of high level communication.

But a person who is dealing with depression symptoms has more power.

My family member is now *acting* as a Toastmasters speaker, and I'm excited for her. I'm proud of her!

"In truth I am a verb." – Steve Chandler

It's easy to categorize ourselves as a "noun" like "depressed person" or "shy person."

It more healthy and strong to identify yourself as a "verb"—your actions can change and with those actions you can grow and increase your happiness.

You are NOT stuck.

Have you noticed how much we, as audience members, like it when heroes in a movie are defiant. I will always remember a scene of the 1986 film, *Highlander*, in which a character (portrayed by Sean Connery) was defiant to the last moments of his life.

In films and plays, we often enjoy seeing a person holding strong and defiant in spite of the odds.

I will always remember the song "Defying Gravity" from the musical play *Wicked*.

A phrase leapt into my thoughts:

I defy in the name of Love-Heart-and-Strength.

Consider how you can defy past, disempowering labels. Choose new actions that help you TODAY.

What past, disempowering labels do you want to free yourself from? What three small actions can you do to go into the direction of becoming stronger and healthier?

_____

_____

_____

_____

_____

_____

_____

_____

_____

Protect and Build Your Energy #14

Get the Breakthrough You Want for Success and Happiness!

"Should I wait one week or two weeks for that potential vendor to get back to me?" I asked my mentor.

She replied, "How about looking for other options?"

A vital part of making your life better is taking action. What works even better is taking Effective Action. And that is what my mentor suggests that I do.

As an Executive Coach, I help clients get into action, reflect and refine each subsequent action. I am an Opti-Realist. That's a vital combination of Optimism and Realism.

When you hire a coach, you have someone totally on your side but who does not have "a horse in the race" like a co-worker or family member. The idea of "a horse in the race" means that the co-worker or family member has their own selfish agenda.

The Executive Coach only focuses on your dreams and your personal growth.

Co-workers/family members may not want to be inconvenienced by necessary changes you're making. They may have their own fears and many suffer from the "crab mentality." Crabs, in a boiling pot, will hold each other down and all die—instead of working to let one get out at a time.

Simply stated, some people get uncomfortable when you're successful near them.

An Executive Coach further helps you find the Right Questions so you leap forward in your life.

I help my clients with the M.A.P. Process:

M – measure
A – adjust
P – purpose-focus

1. Measure

How do you know that you're taking action in effective ways? Measure what you're doing and what results you're getting.

Here's a simple example: If you have started a company and need to get clients through phone conversations, measure how many phone calls you make. Some people discover that they need to make 25 phone calls to make one sale. As they improve in their phone/selling skills, the ratio can improve: 15 calls to make one sale.

Make the measurement simple and clear.

Some examples:
- phone calls made today
- emails sent today
- thank you notes sent via the Postal Service [It's unusual to receive a thank you-card.]

2. Adjust

Sometimes a person or whole team will be in the grip of

an invisible fear. Of what? Loss of Approval. There are times when a goal or project proves to be NOT a match for the marketplace. But people hold the goal in a death grip. They're afraid of looking bad because they had to abandon a faulty goal/project.

Some people merely say, "Double the effort."

On the other hand, perhaps, what is really called for is to adjust the project.

For example, publisher/multi-millionaire Felix Dennis had a team well-skilled in publishing magazines. Then, they started to publish a catalog that failed! No one was buying. Then one woman on the team said, "This doesn't look like a catalog." Felix had the team study other catalogs, and they made big changes. And BAM!—lots of sales.

Merely, "doubling the effort" may be the wrong approach.

You may need to make significant adjustments.

Do not give into the Fear of Loss of Approval. Make the right decision—not just a popular one.

You may be holding the "Wrong B.A.G."

Sometimes, the marketplace may show us that our goal or approach is faulty.

With my clients, I talk about "Beware of B.A.G."—that is, "Blind Adherence to Goal."

As an Executive Coach, my job is to keep my eyes wide open and help clients open their eyes, too.

As we get feedback from the marketplace, we adjust and improve the project. Or even throw out the wrong project. We avoid "Blind Adherence to a Goal."

How do you know?

You use the next step . . .

3. Purpose-focus

I've coined a term "purpose-focus." By this I mean, you return to your Core Values and your Core Desires. What does your heart want?

When working with a client, I help the person focus on what I call Triple-Power:

Work you do well –> people will pay for –> Clients you WANT

If you do something well (for example, poetry) but no one will pay for it, you may want to do it with your other efforts to make a living. (It's an "AND-universe.")

Another vital element is Clients you WANT. Often, I hear people complain about "terrible clients."

I've learned that you can set up your business so you work with Clients you WANT. I have only a few clients whom I coach. I'm so careful about the selection that I talk with their references. Why? I give a significant portion of my time, energy and life to working with a particular client. So I have a process to work only with clients I want.

One author, Rich Litvin, said, "I only coach Kings and Queens." By this, he means he only works with people who take responsibility and who do not get mired in a "blame others pattern." That approach related to "Kings and Queens" is powerful.

I emphasize that the process returns to you taking action, aligned to your heart. This is "purpose-focus."

* * *

This section is about *Get the Breakthrough You Want for Success and Happiness!* I'm often asked by clients to help them come with their niche in business—that is to make a *breakthrough* in their marketing. I introduce them to what I call **"Different, Specific, Authentic (DSA)."**

If one is going to do a workshop, it needs to be

Different – to be unique and rise above the noise in the marketplace

Specific – How will the workshop provide particular benefits?

Authentic – Are you teaching about something you personally went through? Then you can be authentic in teaching this particular workshop.

To make a breakthrough, here's a Helpful Question: **Are you doing what is necessary? What will you change? Are you holding the wrong B.A.G. (Blind Adherence to a Goal)? Are you focusing on your purpose?**

_____

_____

_____

_____

_____

_____

_____

_____

A FINAL WORD AND SPRINGBOARD TO YOUR DREAMS

Congratulations on your efforts as your worked with the material in this book. To get even more value from this book, take the plans and insights that you created and place them in some form in your calendar or day planner. *Plan and take action.* Return to these pages again and again to reconnect with the material and take your life to higher levels.

The best to you,
Tom

Tom Marcoux
Executive Coach - Spoken Word Strategist

Special Offer Just for Readers of this Book:

Contact Tom Marcoux at tomsupercoach@gmail.com for special discounts on **coaching**, books, workshops and presentations. Just mention your experience with this book.

==> See an Excerpt from Tom Marcoux's book, *Darkest Secrets of Persuasion and Seduction Masters: How to Protect Yourself and Turn the Power to Good* – on the next page.

Excerpt from
Darkest Secrets of Persuasion and Seduction Masters: How to Protect Yourself and Turn the Power to Good
by *Tom Marcoux, Executive Coach – Spoken Word Strategist*
Copyright Tom Marcoux

... Now, I am in my 40's, with gray in my hair, and for 27 years I have been taking action to protect people.

And now is the time for me to protect you with the Countermeasures I reveal in this book.

Every human being needs to be able to break the trance that a Manipulator creates.

You need to make good decisions so you are safe and you keep growing—and you are not cut down and crippled.

This Darkest Secrets material is so intense that I first released it only with the counterbalance of my most energizing and uplifting books, *Nothing Can Stop You This Year!* and *10 Seconds to Wealth: Master the Moment Using Your Divine Gifts.*

An interviewer asked me: "Who can be the Manipulator?"

A co-worker, a boss, a salesperson, someone you're dating, and someone you think is a friend.

Now is the time—this very minute—for me to write this book to protect you.

I must speak the truth.

These Darkest Secrets of "persuasion masters" are ...

Wait a minute! Let's say it plainly: These are the Darkest Secrets of masters of manipulation. Throughout this book, I will call these people what they are: Manipulators.

Dictionary.com defines "manipulate" as "To influence or manage shrewdly or deviously.... To tamper with or falsify for personal gain."

In this book, we will look on a manipulator as one who deviously influences someone with no concern about that person's well-being, and who causes harm to that person.

Here is the first Darkest Secret:

Darkest Secret #1:
Manipulators Make You Hurt
and Then Offer the Salve.

Manipulators would invite you to go out in the sun for hours and then sell you the salve to soothe your burns. The problem is that we don't notice that this is what they're doing.

For example, you're considering the purchase of a house. A Manipulator asks the question, "So, where would you put your TV?" This question is designed to put you into a trance.

Dictionary.com defines "trance" as "a half-conscious state, seemingly between sleeping and waking, in which ability to function voluntarily may be suspended." Let's condense this: in a trance you may not be able to function freely.

Here is the second Secret:

Darkest Secret #2:
Manipulators Put You into a Trance.

To protect yourself, you must learn to use Countermeasures to Break the Trance.

All the Countermeasures (actions you can take to break the trance) in this book will make you stronger and more capable of protecting yourself.

Now, we'll view the third Secret:

Darkest Secret #3:
Manipulators Care Nothing for You and Human Decency: They'll lie, cheat, and do whatever they need to do so they win—but their charm masks all this.

Let's return to the example of a Manipulator selling you a house. A Manipulator does not pause for an instant to see if you can truly afford the new house. The Manipulator would neglect to mention that you will not only have your mortgage payment of $900. There will be additional costs: home repairs, property tax, water, electricity, homeowner's insurance, and more. The Manipulator only emphasizes what he or she knows you want to hear: "Look! $900 is better than the $1500 you're paying for rent, which is just going down the toilet. And the $900 is an investment."

Let's go back to **Darkest Secret #1:**
Manipulators make you hurt and then offer the salve.

The Manipulator has you feeling good about the solution (salve) and feeling bad about your current life situation.

How? A Manipulator will make you hurt through questions such as:
- What bothers you about paying $1500 a month for rent?

(The Manipulator will use a derisive tone when he says the word *rent*.)

• What is *not* smart about paying rent on someone else's house instead of investing in your own house?

• How do you feel about your children walking in the neighborhood where you live now?

Do you see how these questions are designed to make you hurt enough so that you'll buy?

An interviewer asked me, "Tom, aren't these good arguments for purchasing a house?"

"What we're looking at is the *intention* of the influencer," I replied. "Let's look at our definition of a manipulator as one who deviously influences someone with no concern about that person's well-being, and who causes harm to that person. If the person truly cannot afford the house, he or she will be harmed by buying it. If the manipulator conceals the truth, the manipulator is doing harm. That's the important difference."

Some friends of mine are ethical and helpful real estate agents who truthfully reveal the whole situation and help the purchaser achieve her own goals.

In this book, we are talking about another type of person; that is, unethical Manipulators.

* * *

In any given moment, we need to remember the tactics Manipulators use. We will focus on the word D.A.R.K. so you can remember details easily and protect yourself from Manipulators.

D — Dangle something for nothing
A — Alert to scarcity

R — Reveal the Desperate Hot Button
K — Keep on pushing buttons

1. Dangle Something for Nothing

What do conmen and conwomen do to seize your attention? They make you think you're getting a "steal."

I recently saw a documentary in which a conman on a street in England showed a toy that looked like it was dancing. This fake product was actually dancing because of a hidden, invisible thread. The conman was dangling something for nothing. The Entranced Buyer thought he was getting something worth $20 for only $5. That was the trick. The Entranced Buyer felt that he was getting $15 extra of value for his $5. What the Buyer really got was something worth nothing. Similarly, I know someone who purchased a copy of a Disney movie from a street vendor in San Francisco. She brought the copy home and it was unwatchable—and the street vendor was never seen again.

An old phrase goes, "A conman cannot con someone who is not looking for something for nothing."

How to Protect Yourself from "Dangle Something for Nothing"

Stop! Get on your cell phone and talk through the "deal" with someone you know who thinks clearly. Go home. Think about it. Do some research on the Internet. Listen to your gut feelings. If the salesman or conman is too insistent, get away from that Manipulator. Get quiet. Have a cup of water. Cool down. Break the Trance!

Break the Trance and Identify the Crucial Detail

Earlier, I mentioned that a Manipulator puts you into a

trance. An added problem is that we put ourselves into a trance. For example, as you read this, are you thinking about your right toe? Most likely not (unless you stubbed your toe recently). The point is that we only focus on a tiny percentage of what is going on in our life.

Around fifteen years ago, I caused myself trouble because I put myself into a trance. I discovered that under certain conditions, friendship can make you nearly deaf. Here's how: I was producing a song for a motion picture. A good friend was singing backup in the chorus. Because of our friendship, I wanted him to sound great. I completely missed the Crucial Detail. In this kind of situation, the Crucial Detail is that what truly counts is how the lead singer sounds! I made a song that I could not release. What a waste of time and money! I had put myself into a trance.

In any situation in which the Manipulator is "dangling something for nothing," we often fall into a trance and miss the Crucial Detail. The most important detail is *not* that we're saving money if we order before midnight tonight. What counts is whether the product creates a lasting, crucial benefit in our lives. And is the benefit of the product worth the cost? Some people even program themselves to make mistakes by saying, "I can't pass up a bargain." The bargain is *not* the Crucial Detail.

Secrets to Break the Trance

This is the process of B.R.E.A.K.S. It will help you remember the proven methods to break a trance.

B — Breathe
R — Relax
E — Envision

A — Act on aromas
K — Keep moving
S — Smile

Secret #1: Breathe

Remember Secret #1: Manipulators make you hurt and then offer the salve. The Manipulator wants to put you into a state of being that fills you with a sense of urgency and anxiety. Oh, no! I'm going to miss the sale!

Stop this highly vulnerable state. Take a deep breath. Do it now. Take a deep breath and let your belly "get fat" by filling it with air. As you breathe out, let your belly deflate. Breathe in through your nose and breathe out through your mouth. This is called belly-breathing. Repeat the actions of belly-breathing three times. Good. Now, do you feel different? Remember, when you are relaxed, you are strong.

Secret #2: Relax

You become stronger when you condition yourself to relax in the face of adversity. Researchers note that when an Olympic athlete is confronted with the most stressful moment in her life, she has prepared in advance. She has given herself ways to calm down. Two powerful methods are described in this section about B.R.E.A.K.S. One is breathing, and the other is envisioning.

A special part of relaxing is the effective use of your posture. Many of us think that we're relaxed when we slouch. However, I was taught by three physical therapists that when you sit up and align your vertebrae, you are more relaxed because your back's bone structure is naturally supporting you. Many of us discover that placing a pillow behind the lumbar-area of our back helps us sit up better. If you are sitting or standing when talking with a Manipulator, ensure that your posture is aligned. You will have more power to protect yourself.

Secret #3: Envision

Envision an image that makes you feel strong. Often, our strongest images come from movies that we saw when we were young. Some of my clients envision being strong like Xena the Warrior Princess or Superman. One client thinks of Sean Connery as James Bond. Immediately, this client walks smoothly with poise. He feels confident. Act as if you are, and you are!

Also, envision yourself being quite aware of your surroundings. On vacation, many of us become entranced by our new surroundings. Travelers let their guard down. A conperson catches them at a weak moment. It's important to stay in the present and be alert to what's going on. Stay present with your needs, and shop around before making a large purchase. Be prepared to walk away.

Watch out for Manipulators who are slick, fast talkers. They try to get your money, and just minutes after they succeed, you realize what happened.

But this is *not* for you! You can remind yourself with an internal comment: "I am aware. What is really going on here?"

Secret #4: Act on Aromas

Let's notice the power of an aroma.

Smell is a potent wizard that transports you across thousands of miles and all the years you have lived. – Helen Keller

Nothing is more memorable than a smell. One scent can be unexpected, momentary and fleeting, yet conjure up a childhood

summer beside a lake in the mountains. – Diane Ackerman

You need to be able to calm down within seconds. One of the fastest ways to do that is to use a favorite aroma. One of my clients has conditioned herself to calm down by smelling lavender. The process for her was to recline in a hot bath and smell lavender simultaneously. Now, the smell of lavender relaxes her limbs quickly.

Remember, when you are relaxed, you neutralize the Manipulator's tactic to make you feel that buying something now is an urgent matter. You let go of any anxious feelings the Manipulator seeks to create in you. Use an aroma to help you feel relaxed and strong.

Secret #5: Keep Moving

A trance often transfixes or freezes us, making us still. Sometimes, the most powerful way to break a trance is to use a movement that you prepared in advance. One of my clients closes his right fist and taps it on his right thigh. In his mind, he repeats the phrase: "I am my own person!" This helps him break out of a trance induced by a Manipulator.

Another client quietly snaps her fingers near her waist. This reminds her to "snap out of it."

Excerpt from
Darkest Secrets of Persuasion and Seduction Masters: How to Protect Yourself and Turn the Power to Good

Purchase your copy of this book (paperback or ebook) at Amazon.com or BarnesandNoble.com
See **Free Chapters** of Tom Marcoux's 31 books at http://amzn.to/ZiCTRj

ABOUT THE AUTHOR

You want more and better, right? Imagine fulfilling your Big Dream.

Tom Marcoux can help you—in that he's coached thousands of people: CEOs, small business leaders, graduate students (at Stanford University) speakers, and authors.

Marcoux is known as an effective **Executive Coach** and **Spoken Word Strategist.**

(and Thought Leader—okay, writing 31 books helped with that!)

** *CEOs, Vice-Presidents, Other Executives, Small Business Leaders:*

You know that leading people and speaking at your best can be tough.

Marcoux solves problems while helping you amplify your own Charisma, Confidence and Control of Time.

Interested? Email Marcoux—tomsupercoach@gmail.com

Ask for a *Special Report:*

* 9 Deadly Mistakes to Avoid for Your Next Speech

** *Speakers, Experts - for a great TED Talk, Book, Audio Book, Speeches, YouTube Videos.*

Marcoux solve problems while helping you to make your

Concise, Compelling Message that gets people to trust you and get what you're offering (product, service, *an idea*).

Yes - the *San Francisco Examiner* designated Tom Marcoux as "The Personal Branding Instructor."

Marcoux is an expert on STORY. He won a Special Award at the EMMY AWARDS, and he directed a feature film that went to the CANNES FILM MARKET and earned international distribution.

(Marcoux helps you *Be Heard and Be Trusted* . . . that's his 15th Anniversary, 3rd edition book.)

As a CEO, Marcoux leads teams in the United Kingdom, India and the USA. Marcoux guides clients & audiences (IBM, Sun MicroSystems, etc.) in leadership, team-building, power time management and branding. See Tom's Popular BLOG: www.TomSuperCoach.com

Specialties: coach to CEOS * Executives * Small Business owners * Leaders * Speakers * Experts * Authors * Academics

One of his *Darkest Secrets* books rose to #1 on Amazon.com Hot New Releases in Business Life (and in Business Communication). A member of the National Speakers Association for over 14 years, he is a professional coach and guest expert on TV, radio, and print.

Marcoux addressed National Association of Broadcasters' Conference six years running. With a degree in psychology, Tom is a guest lecturer at **Stanford University**, DeAnza, & California State University, and teaches business communication, designing careers, public speaking, science fiction cinema/literature and comparative religion at Academy of Art University. He is engaged in book/film projects *Crystal Pegasus* (children's) and *Jack AngelSword* (thriller-fantasy). See Tom's well-received blogs

at www.BeHeardandBeTrusted.com

at www.YourBodySoulandProsperity.com

Consider engaging **Tom Marcoux as your Executive Coach.**

"As Tom's client for many years, I have benefited from his wisdom and strategic approach. Do your career and personal life a big favor and get his books and engage him as your Executive Coach." – Dr. JoAnn Dahlkoetter, author of *Your Performing Edge* and Coach to CEOs and Olympic Gold Medalists

"Tom Marcoux coached me to get more done in 10 days than other coaches in 2 years." – Brad Carlson, CEO of MindStrong LLC

Tom Marcoux can help you with **speech writing** and **coaching for your best performance.**
As Tom says, *Make Your Speech a Pleasant Beach.*
Join Tom's Linkedin.com group: *Executive Public Speaking and Communication Power.*
At Google+: join the community "Create Your Best Life – Charisma & Confidence"
Get a **Free** report: "9 Deadly Mistakes to Avoid for Your Next Speech and 9 Surefire Methods" at
http://tomsupercoach.com/freereport9Mistakes4Speech.html

Tom Marcoux has trained CEOs, small business owners, and graduate students to speak with impact and gain audiences' tremendous approval and cooperation. *Learn how to present and get thunderous applause!*
"Tom, Thanks for your coaching and work with me on revising my speech at a major university. Working with you has been so enlightening for me. Through your gentle prodding and guidance I was able to write a speech that connects with the audience. I wish everyone could experience the transformation I have undergone. You have helped me discover the warm and compelling stories that now make my speech reach hearts and uplift minds. This was truly an empowering experience. I cannot thank you enough for your great assistance." – J.S.

"Tom Marcoux has been an NAB Conference favorite [speaker] for six years. And he is very energetic."

– John Marino, Vice President, National Association of Broadcasters, Washington, D.C.

"Using just one of Tom Marcoux's methods, I got more done in 2 weeks than in 6 months."

– Jaclyn Freitas, M.A.

Tom's Coaching features innovations:
- Dynamic Rehearsal
- Power Rehearsal for Crisis
- The Charisma Advantage that Saves You Time

Become a fan of Tom's graphic novels/feature films:
- Fantasy Thriller: *Jack AngelSword*
  type "JackAngelSword" at Facebook.com
- Science fiction: *TimePulse*
  www.facebook.com/timepulsegraphicnovel
- Children's Fantasy: *Crystal Pegasus*
  www.facebook.com/crystalpegasusandrose

See **Free Chapters** of Tom Marcoux's 31 books at http://amzn.to/ZiCTRj   Amazon.com

Your Notes:

_____

_____

_____

Your Notes:

www.ingramcontent.com/pod-product-compliance
Lightning Source LLC
Chambersburg PA
CBHW070456100426
42743CB00010B/1647